THE COMPLETE IDIOT'S GUIDE® TO

Geocaching

2nd Edition

by The Editors and Staff of Geocaching.com

ALPHA

A member of Penguin Group (USA) Inc.

ALPHA BOOKS

Published by the Penguin Group

Penguin Group (USA) Inc., 375 Hudson Street, New York, New York 10014, USA

Penguin Group (Canada), 90 Eglinton Avenue East, Suite 700, Toronto, Ontario M4P 2Y3, Canada (a division of Pearson Penguin Canada Inc.)

Penguin Books Ltd., 80 Strand, London WC2R 0RL, England

Penguin Ireland, 25 St. Stephen's Green, Dublin 2, Ireland (a division of Penguin Books Ltd.)

Penguin Group (Australia), 250 Camberwell Road, Camberwell, Victoria 3124, Australia (a division of Pearson Australia Group Pty. Ltd.)

Penguin Books India Pvt. Ltd., 11 Community Centre, Panchsheel Park, New Delhi—110 017, India

Penguin Group (NZ), 67 Apollo Drive, Rosedale, North Shore, Auckland 1311, New Zealand (a division of Pearson New Zealand Ltd.)

Penguin Books (South Africa) (Pty.) Ltd., 24 Sturdee Avenue, Rosebank, Johannesburg 2196, South Africa

Penguin Books Ltd., Registered Offices: 80 Strand, London WC2R 0RL, England

Copyright © 2009 by The Editors and Staff of Geocaching.com

International Standard Book Number: 978-1-59257-877-1
Library of Congress Catalog Card Number: 2008939796

12   11   10   8   7   6   5

Interpretation of the printing code: The rightmost number of the first series of numbers is the year of the book's printing; the rightmost number of the second series of numbers is the number of the book's printing. For example, a printing code of 09-1 shows that the first printing occurred in 2009.

Printed in the United States of America

Note: This publication contains the opinions and ideas of its authors. It is intended to provide helpful and informative material on the subject matter covered. It is sold with the understanding that the authors and publisher are not engaged in rendering professional services in the book. If the reader requires personal assistance or advice, a competent professional should be consulted.

The authors and publisher specifically disclaim any responsibility for any liability, loss, or risk, personal or otherwise, which is incurred as a consequence, directly or indirectly, of the use and application of any of the contents of this book.

Most Alpha books are available at special quantity discounts for bulk purchases for sales promotions, premiums, fund-raising, or educational use. Special books, or book excerpts, can also be created to fit specific needs.

For details, write: Special Markets, Alpha Books, 375 Hudson Street, New York, NY 10014.

Publisher: *Marie Butler-Knight*

Associate Publisher: *Mike Sanders*

Senior Managing Editor: *Billy Fields*

Acquisitions Editor: *Tom Stevens*

Development Editor: *Jennifer Bowles*

Senior Production Editor: *Janette Lynn*

Copy Editor: *Jennifer Connolly*

Cover Designer: *William Thomas*

Book Designer: *William Thomas, Rebecca Batchelor*

Indexer: *Tonya Heard*

Layout: *Rebecca Batchelor*

Proofreader: *Laura Caddell*

Contents

Appendixes

Introduction

Congratulations for taking the time to find this book, *The Complete Idiot's Guide to Geocaching, Second Edition.* Here is your opportunity to learn about one of the most exciting and fastest growing recreational activities in the world. Since the release of the first edition of this book, recreational use of GPS technology has grown significantly on a global scale. Within geocaching, many things have changed and many things have remained the same. People around the world continue taking time out of their busy schedules to head outdoors and enjoy themselves. They are spending time in parks and on the trail with friends and family, and for many, it has introduced them to outdoor recreation for the first time. Over the past eight years, geocaching has become extremely popular because it enables people to embrace both technology and the outdoors in one activity.

Our goal in writing this second edition was to create the next version of the ultimate book on geocaching: one that makes learning about the activity enjoyable and easy to understand. Whether you are new to geocaching or a seasoned veteran, we trust you'll find that we've covered all of the topics necessary to keep you geocaching successfully and safely every time you hit the trail. This is no easy endeavor. Although this is the second version of an original, and the official book of Geocaching.com, the activity has changed significantly throughout the years. In many cases, we found ourselves starting from scratch and covering new aspects of the activity that were not present at the time the first edition was written.

What You'll Learn in This Book

In our effort to make this book user-friendly, we have divided the chapters into five parts.

Part 1, "Welcome to Geocaching," covers the basics of what geocaching is and how it all got started. We go over the game's limited rules and offer information and advice to help you get started. We explain how to participate and prepare for outdoor geocaching adventures. We also explain Global Positioning System (GPS) technology, which makes geocaching possible.

Part 2, "Get Out and Play," gets down to the business of playing the game. We explore how to find geocaches to seek on the Geocaching.com website. Then, we teach you how to get outside and find geocaches in the real world. We cover everything you need to know in order to find the most difficult of geocaches, and then discuss how to hide your own for others to find. In Part 2, you'll also discover the fun of Travel Bugs and other trackable items.

Part 3, "Get in Gear," teaches you all about GPS devices, including their features and functions, so that you'll have a solid understanding of what GPS technology can do. You learn about available GPS receiver options so that you can purchase the right unit for your use, and we explain how to set up your unit so that you'll be ready to hit the trail. Finally, we unravel some of the mystery behind GPS mapping and computers.

Part 4, "Welcome to the Community," introduces you to the worldwide geocaching community. We teach you about the tools currently used for community interaction and show you how to find answers to any questions you have. We introduce you to the discussion forums, geocaching organizations, and geocaching events around the world. We also provide you with some information on geocaching while traveling, including tips for fun and safety.

Part 5, "The Future of GPS Games," presents some new GPS-based entertainment concepts, including waymarking and Wherigo. We explain how geocaching can be taken to the next level with multimedia experiences and unique locations in the world. Finally, we discuss the future of geocaching and GPS and provide you with insight on how you can be a part of the revolution that will make geocaching fun for generations to come.

Extras

We've added these extras to help you navigate through the world of GPS and geocaching. Keep a lookout for Signal, the Groundspeak Frog, for a fun way to learn important tips, geocaching language, and warnings.

EUREKA!

These provide tips, discoveries, and trivia.

GEO-LINGO

These help define technical or slang terminology.

NAVIGATIONAL NUGGETS

These provide useful advice specific to GPS and navigation.

DEAD BATTERIES

These provide a caution or warning to help keep you out of trouble.

Acknowledgments

This project took a lot of work and there are a few people to thank for helping to make this book possible. First, a special thanks to Jack Peters who authored the first edition. Much of what you read here has been built upon Jack's original work and research. Thank you to Bret Hammond, one of the contributing editors on this second edition. Bret contributed his many years of geocaching knowledge and insight to this book while he spent countless hours reviewing and editing the content. Thank you to Shauna Maggs, a contributing editor and Groundspeak's director of marketing. Although she is included in the list of Groundspeak staff, Shauna sacrificed countless nights and weekends to make sure that this book met with our highest of expectations. Also, thanks go to Tom Stevens and the rest of the staff and editors at Penguin Group (USA) Inc./Alpha Books. Their follow-through and patience made this book possible. Always, thanks to our family and friends for your assistance, patience, and support. We could not have done it without you. Finally, thank you to the many volunteers and geocachers around the world who have made geocaching possible. We are continually inspired by your passion and dedication to geocaching, and it is truly an honor to serve you.

Trademarks

All terms mentioned in this book that are known to be or are suspected of being trademarks or service marks have been appropriately capitalized. Groundspeak, Alpha Books, and Penguin Group (USA) Inc. cannot attest to the accuracy of this information. Use of a term in this book should not be regarded as affecting the validity of any trademark or service mark.

Welcome to Geocaching

Before you set off to find your first geocache, let's take time to learn about the activity. Geocaching has been around long enough to develop its own traditions, guidelines, and lingo. And even though GPS technology makes staying found easy enough, it's good to understand how it works before depending on it outdoors.

In Part 1, we cover the basics of geocaching—what it is and how it all got started. We explain how to participate and prepare for outdoor geocaching adventures, regardless of whether you're a newbie or a seasoned pro.

We also explain the technology behind geocaching. GPS, the Global Positioning System that enables us to find our way anywhere in the world, makes geocaching possible. We discuss its benefits and limitations so that you can learn to use your gear to its fullest potential.

What Is Geocaching?

In This Chapter

- An explanation of geocaching
- Learn how it all got started
- Big family adventures on a baby budget
- Reasons to play and skills to learn
- What types of geocaches are out there?

The scientists who developed Global Positioning System (GPS) technology probably never thought it would develop into a worldwide activity, but that is exactly what happened. Geocaching is one of the most exciting and quickly growing activities in recent history. But is it a game, a sport, or a relaxing and scenic family activity? It is all of these things, depending on how and where you play and the energy you put into it.

History has demonstrated that people have always had a desire to seek out hidden treasure. Books are filled with stories of lost cities and hidden gold, with people driven to cross oceans, deserts, jungles, and continents in search of the elusive "X" that marks the spot. In this regard, it is not surprising that geocaching is growing in popularity. Considered a modern-day treasure hunt, geocaching helps people experience the outdoors in a way that captures this historical desire for adventure while having fun with friends and family.

This chapter introduces you to geocaching, how it all got started, and how you can begin to participate in this growing, global activity!

This is a typical geocache with a logbook and its treasure stored in a watertight container.
(Geocaching.com)

What Is Geocaching Anyway?

Geocaching combines *geo* for Earth and *cache*, a term used for both hidden provisions and, in a more modern sense, data stored on a computer. Put them together and you have a unique outdoor activity. Enthusiasm for the game has quickly spread as participants combine their love of the great outdoors with their interest in modern technology. It isn't often when you can tap into an outdoor game that has a government budget of more than half a billion dollars a year!

The activity began after the Clinton administration removed selective availability from GPS in May 2000. That was the scrambling technique that made GPS receivers inaccurate up to 100 meters (300 feet). Now that receivers are accurate within 15 meters 90 percent of the time, it is possible to navigate to a specific location with more precision.

As of this writing, geocaching is played all around the globe. There are over 3 million participants worldwide seeking more than 700,000 active geocaches. The number of geocaches continues to grow at a rapid rate as more people share unique locations around the world. It's fun to have a look to see how many geocaches are located within your own backyard. You'll undoubtedly be surprised at the number out there just waiting to be discovered.

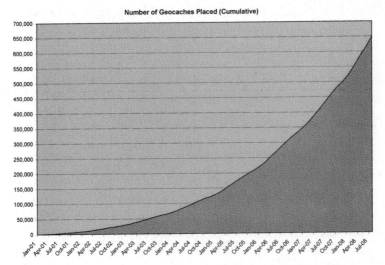

This graph shows the popularity of geocaching since its beginnings in May 2000.
(Geocaching.com)

The goal of geocaching is to locate hidden containers, called *geo-caches,* using latitude/longitude coordinates found on websites, such as Geocaching.com. Geocaches must be watertight to withstand the elements. Items in a geocache are also usually stored in zippered plastic bags to provide additional protection from inclement weather. Geocaches are hidden in the wilderness, parks, or even urban locations accessible to the public. How geocaches are hidden depends on the skill and creativity of the one doing the hiding. Some are easy to find, while others take some work. They could be on a cliff, hidden in a hollow log, even underwater. A geocache is even rated for how difficult it is to find and the type of terrain you must cover to get there. With such a large variety of geocaches and a creative geocaching community, there are unique geocaches available for anyone to find.

 GEO-LINGO

A **geocache** is a container that includes, at a minimum, a logbook for geocachers to sign. Geocaches are not buried but are hidden in plain sight.

Treasure (those items found within a geocache) can include nearly anything of value. Common items are books, toys, tools, games, camping gear, trackable items (more on that later), and sometimes even cash. Successful seekers take something, leave something else, and then sign the cache's logbook. As much fun as it is to find treasure, many geocachers find that the reward is more in the challenge and adventure of locating the geocache.

What's the point, you may ask? Doesn't GPS take you to the exact location? Yes and no. Actually finding a location in the outdoors is often more difficult than it sounds. Going to a geocache's coordinates will take you to the approximate location, but not exactly, due to the system's inaccuracy. Remember, a GPS receiver is accurate to about 15 meters, or 49 feet, most of the time. Using a high-end GPS receiver and assuming the receiver has a clear view of the sky, accuracy can range between 5 to 10 meters. That's as low as 17 feet on a good day! However, in thinking about accuracy, you must also consider the receiver of the person who hid the geocache. How accurate was her device and were there conditions that would further impact accuracy, such as weather or tree cover? The bottom line is that you may have more area to cover than you originally anticipate, and that can be a lot of rocks, trees, and benches to look around.

Geocaching websites like Geocaching.com provide you with the coordinates of the geocache, but not how to get there. The person who hid the first geocache of record, David Ulmer, reminds us that there are 360 ways to get to any one location. Roads on a map may not be accessible, and a map may not show the difficulty of the terrain.

After a geocache has been found, or not, seekers can post feedback, or logs describing their geocaching experiences. These postings are fun to read, often provide clues for other geocachers, and are a way to document previous adventures. Persons posting comments should be careful not to post spoilers by giving too much information and making it too easy for the next person, such as saying, "We couldn't find it until we looked on the south side of the big tree!"

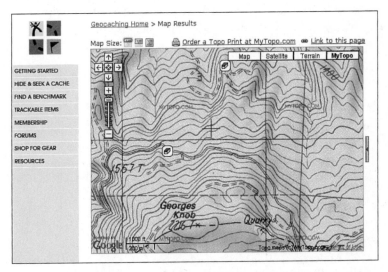

This Google map shows a geocache located near a dashed line representing an unimproved road.
(Geocaching.com)

This map is an example of the maps available from the Geocaching. com website. This map shows the "A Road Less Traveled By" geocache placed in Oregon by a geocacher who uses the name "Odder." Finding this cache requires off-road driving or hiking to get to this remote location.

As geocaching has grown, certain standards and guidelines have come into place to protect players and the environment, while still allowing a lot of creativity on the part of geocache placers. The game is quickly making its way into the mainstream of outdoor activities with many outdoor groups and even tourism bureaus using geocaching as a fun way to get people outside and exploring the world around them.

How It All Got Started

Geocaching can definitely be considered a product of the new millennium. With the limited accuracy of available GPS signals prior to 2000, geocaching would have been much too difficult. A GPS receiver would get you only so close to the cache and then you'd have to spend a lot of time searching a broad area. After the removal of *selective availability* in 2000, the resulting increase in accuracy combined with some creative thinking on the part of some individuals led to the beginning of geocaching.

 GEO-LINGO

Selective availability (SA) was an intentional error in GPS technology. When turned on, accuracy of GPS was around 300 feet. It would be like trying to find and catch a hopping "You are here" sign in an area the size of a football field. Today's receiver accuracy typically ranges from 16 to 49 feet.

GPS Users Get an Instant Upgrade

On May 2, 2000, at approximately midnight, eastern daylight saving time, the system controlling selective availability was changed. Twenty-four satellites around the globe processed their new orders, and instantly the accuracy of GPS technology improved tenfold. Tens of thousands of GPS receivers around the world had an instant upgrade.

The announcement a day before came as a welcome surprise to everyone who worked with GPS technology. The government had planned to remove selective availability—but had until 2006 to do so. Now, said the White House, anyone could "precisely pinpoint their location or the location of items left behind for later recovery." How right they were.

London, Paris, New York, Beaver Creek?

For GPS enthusiasts, the removal of selective availability was definitely a cause for celebration. Internet newsgroups suddenly teemed with ideas about how the technology could be used.

Dave Ulmer, a computer consultant, wanted to test this accuracy by hiding a navigational target in the woods. He called his idea the "Great American GPS Stash Hunt" and posted it on an Internet GPS users' group. The idea was simple: Hide a container out in the woods and note the coordinates with a GPS unit. The finder would then have to locate the container with only the use of his GPS receiver. The rules for the finder were simple: "Take some stuff, leave some stuff."

On May 3, 2000, Ulmer placed his own container, a black bucket, in the woods near Beaver Creek, Oregon. Along with a logbook and pencil, he left various prize items including videos, books, software, and a slingshot. He shared the location of his "stash" with a users' group in the online community:

N 45 17.460°　Latitude　　　W 122 24.800°　Longitude

Within three days, two different individuals read about his stash on the Internet, used their own GPS receivers to find the container, and shared their experiences online. Throughout the next week, others excited by the prospect of hiding and finding stashes began hiding their own containers and posting coordinates. Like many new and innovative ideas on the Internet, the concept spread quickly—but this one required actually leaving your computer to participate.

EUREKA!

Due to the global nature of geocaching, there are various pronunciations of the term. However, the most common pronunciation is jee-oh-kash-ing, like riding in a Jeep and cashing a check.

Within the first month, Mike Teague, the first person to find Ulmer's stash, began gathering the online posts of coordinates around the world and documenting them on his personal web page. The GPS Stash Hunt mailing list was created to discuss this emerging activity. Names were even tossed about to replace the name "stash" due to the negative connotations associated with that name. One such name was "geocaching."

The Origins of "Geocaching"

Geocaching, first coined by Matt Stum on the GPS Stash Hunt mailing list on May 30, 2000, was the joining of two familiar words. The prefix, *geo*, for Earth, was used to describe the global nature of the activity, but also for its use in familiar topics in GPS such as geography.

Caching, from the word *cache*, has two different uses, which makes it very appropriate for the activity. A French word invented in 1797, the original definition referred to a hiding place someone would use to temporarily store items. The word *cache* stirs up visions of pioneers, gold miners, and even pirates. Today the word is still used in the news to describe hidden weapon locations.

The second use of *cache* has more recently been used in technology. *Memory cache* is computer storage that is used to quickly retrieve frequently used information. Your web browser, for example, stores images on disk so you don't have to retrieve the same image every time you visit similar pages.

The combination of Earth, hiding, and technology made *geocaching* an excellent term for the activity. However, the GPS Stash Hunt was the original and most widely used term until Mike Teague passed the torch to Jeremy Irish in September 2000.

The Birth of Geocaching.com

For the first few months, geocaching was confined to existing, experienced GPS users who already used the technology for outdoor activities such as backpacking and boating. Most participants had an existing knowledge of GPS and a firm grasp of obscure lingo such as "datums" and "WGS84." Due to both the experienced player base and the newness of the activity, new players had a steep learning curve before going out on their first cache hunt. Tools were scarce for determining whether a cache was nearby, if one existed at all.

As with most participants, Jeremy Irish, a web developer for a Seattle company, stumbled upon Mike Teague's website in July while doing research on GPS technology. The idea of treasure hunting and using tech gadgets represented the marriage of two of his biggest interests. Discovering that one was hidden nearby, Irish purchased his first GPS unit and went on his first hunt the following weekend.

After experiencing the thrill of finding his first geocache, Irish decided to start a hobby site for the activity. Adopting the term "geocaching," he created Geocaching.com and applied his professional web skills to create tools to improve the cache-hunting experience. The cache listings were still added by hand, but a database helped to standardize the listings, and features such as searching for caches around zip codes made it easier for new players to find listings for nearby caches.

With Mike Teague's valuable input, the new site was completed and announced to the stash-hunting community on September 2, 2000. At the time the site was launched, there were 75 known geocaches in the world.

If You Hide It, They Will Come

Slashdot, a popular online magazine for techies, reported the new activity on September 25, 2000, introducing a larger group of technology professionals to the activity. *The New York Times* picked up the story and featured it in its "Circuits" section in October, starting a domino effect of articles written in magazines, newspapers, and other media outlets around the world. CNN even did a segment in December to profile the new hobby.

EUREKA!

"SD #1" was hidden on March 3, 2001, in South Dakota, the last state in the United States to get a hidden geocache. The eighth finder discovered it in January 2002. After that discovery, the geocache went missing and its maintainer retired it. It can still be found in the archives at Geocaching. com.

However, because there were so few geocaches in the world, many would-be participants discovered they didn't have a cache listed nearby. Many wondered whether anyone would bother looking for a cache if they hid one in the area. The growing community chanted the mantra "If you hide it, they will come" to the newer players. After some reassurances, pioneers of the hobby started placing caches just to see whether people would go find them. They did.

Through word of mouth, press articles, and even accidental cache discoveries, more and more people have become involved in geocaching. First started by technology and GPS enthusiasts, the ranks of geocachers now include couples, families, and groups from all walks of life. The excitement of the hunt appeals to both the inner and outer child. Today you can do a search on just about anywhere in the world and be able to walk, bike, or drive to a nearby hidden cache.

Since Geocaching.com's creation, geocaching has doubled in participants approximately every year. When the website was launched, the pioneers of the game probably never imagined what an international phenomenon geocaching would become. As they say, the rest is history.

Timing Is Everything

Sometimes, multiple factors have to come together in just the right way at just the right time for a new phenomenon to be created. How else could we explain the immediate popularity of geocaching? If you think about it, it all makes sense. Our traditional sports were created around 100 years ago in a low-tech, agricultural, and industrial age. Now, children grow up playing video games and operating computers. Most of the population utilizes technology for work, entertainment, and convenience.

As children, we grow up with a sense of adventure in finding something. From our earliest memories, we recall hunting Easter eggs and hearing stories of pirate's treasure. We enjoy games like hide-and-seek and capture the flag. We live in a unique time when we experience technology that quickly develops from an obscure concept to a daily necessity. Consider the last 20 years, with the rise of personal computers, cell phones, GPS, and the Internet. We can only imagine what's next, and we often wonder how we got by without this gadgetry before.

But along with the rise of technology, we have witnessed the rise of various extreme sports. Adrenaline junkies push themselves to the limits of their abilities and common sense for bragging rights. That is why the time is so right for a game like geocaching. We get to utilize the latest technological advancements in navigation and the web, and challenge our mind, body, and spirit with the childlike excitement of uncovering hidden treasures.

A Hobby, Game, or Sport?

Geocaching can be played anytime, as often as you like. You can do it by yourself or with friends and family. After you get the hang of using GPS and finding caches, you'll enjoy sharing your adventures with fellow geocachers on the web, or better yet, in person. Geocaching events are held throughout the world and are a way in which people can get together to discuss geocaching.

Cache Me If You Can

Because this game is so innovative and continues to evolve, you cannot expect it to be a one-cache-fits-all kind of game. You need to be aware of a number of different kinds of geocaches before selecting one to find for yourself. Common geocache types include …

- **Traditional Cache.** This is the original cache type consisting of, at a bare minimum, a container and a logbook. Normally you'll find a tupperware container, ammo box, or bucket filled with goodies. A smaller container (known as a "micro cache") is too small to contain items except for a logbook and usually requires you to bring your own pen. The coordinates listed on the traditional cache page are the exact location for the cache.

- **Multi-Cache.** A multi-cache ("multiple") involves two or more locations, the final location being a physical container. There are many variations, but most multi-caches have a hint to find the second cache, and the second cache has hints to the third, and so on. An offset cache (where you go to a location and get hints to the actual cache) is considered a multi-cache.

- **Mystery or Puzzle Caches.** The catchall of cache types, this form of cache can involve complicated puzzles you first need to solve to determine the coordinates. It might also involve performing some task at the cache location and taking a photograph, or writing the online log in a format or with content that satisfies the cache requirements. Due to the increasing creativity of geocaching, this becomes the staging ground for new and unique challenges.

- **Letterbox Hybrid.** A letterbox is another form of treasure hunting using clues instead of coordinates. In some cases, however, a letterbox has coordinates, and the owner has made it a letterbox *and* a geocache.

- **EarthCache.** An EarthCache is a special place that people can visit to learn about a unique geoscience feature or aspect of our Earth. EarthCaches include a set of educational notes and the details about where to find the location (latitude and longitude). Visitors to EarthCaches can see how our planet has been shaped by geological processes, how we manage the resources, and how scientists gather evidence to learn about the Earth. The Geological Society of America (GSA) administers the listing of EarthCache sites around the world on Geocaching.com.

As geocaching matures as an activity, new variations of geocaches continue to be created. At the same time, some cache types are no longer being developed but are still available to be found. These include virtual caches, where the goal is to find a location rather than a container, and webcam caches that use existing web cameras around the world to log a visit. These types of caches helped spur the development of a new activity called "Waymarking," which will be discussed in Chapter 15.

The Geocaching Community

People who play this game—whether alone, with a family, or in a group—consider themselves part of a community. The geocaching community extends from a local bunch of friends and families across the country and around the world. Organizations and groups have sprung up everywhere. You most likely have a group nearby, or at least in your state. These groups often have elaborate websites, and the members get together frequently for all kinds of events, or at least pizza.

The community is made up of adventurers from all walks of life, races, ages, and sexes, loosely bound to each other by their common interest: to enjoy and promote an activity they love so much. What that means to you is that no matter where you travel, if you are a geocacher, you can always make a new friend and have a geocache or two to find.

This is a player-driven and self-regulated activity in which participants take pride in its positive reputation. It is important to always obtain permission from the landowner or managing agency prior to placing your geocache. Also, never place a cache in any area that would be considered a potential environmental hazard, such as in a bed of flowers or rare plants. Caches that are hidden in potentially environment-damaging areas might tarnish the excellent reputation geocachers enjoy and make it more difficult for geocachers to work with park agencies and officials to obtain permission for future cache placements.

It is also important to remember this is a family activity, so nothing should be placed that is considered harmful, illegal, or in bad taste. Geocaching.com will not knowingly post caches that are in inappropriate areas or are filled with illegal or hazardous contents.

The Complete Idiot's Top Ten Reasons to Go Geocaching

10. It's a great excuse to use all that outdoor gear.

9. It's a fun way to learn GPS, navigation, and outdoor skills.

8. It can be exciting to feel like a secret agent.

7. Finding a remote geocache with a loved one can be very romantic.

6. You'll get some exercise, and it's more fun than dieting.

5. You can entertain yourself on the cheap.

4. You can do something together with the whole family.

3. It's a great way to make new friends.

2. You will see places you never knew existed.

1. You get to go outside and play!

The Least You Need to Know

- Geocaching involves finding someone else's hidden treasure using a GPS receiver and your detective skills.
- Geocaching has only been around since 2000, but there are thousands of geocaches hidden all around the world.
- Geocaching is a great activity to get you outdoors, anytime, anywhere.
- Geocaching is fun for the whole family and can be played on a budget.

Game Basics

In This Chapter

- How do you play this game?
- Learn the lingo
- One man's garage sale is another man's treasure
- Geocaching environments
- Grab your gear!

In this chapter, you'll learn the basics of the game and a little about how to speak the language. We'll familiarize you with website features to get you started with your first geocache adventure. We'll cover the environments caches are found in and how to prepare for a successful outdoor trip. Did you know that geocachers have designated their own radio frequencies? Read on, you are getting closer to hitting the trail!

Game Basics

One of the great things about geocaching is it can be as simple or as complicated as you make it. If you're just interested in getting outside with your GPS then you will have a great time. If you're heavily into technology and mapping then there are many resources you can easily employ to make the game what you want it to be. The guidelines that direct the game are written to maximize flexibility and fun.

The basics of the game are simple: The participants select a cache from a geocaching website such as Geocaching.com. After a cache is selected, the coordinates to the location are entered or downloaded into a GPS receiver. It is then up to the players to use their navigational and detective skills to seek out the hidden container.

This is all possible with help from above. The GPS satellites in space broadcast coded signals right to your receiver. A receiver needs to read signals from at least three satellites at a time to calculate its general location through a process called trilateration. Once the receiver knows its position, the receiver can calculate your speed, *bearing*, distance traveled, distance to your destination, and more.

GEO-LINGO

A **bearing** (also known as azimuth), is a compass degree to be followed to find your target. When we go after a geocache, our GPS receiver provides a bearing as one of a compass's 360 degrees.

With signals from four satellites, a GPS receiver can get a more accurate fix that includes altitude and the exact time, as well as latitude and longitude. The more satellite signals the receiver reads, the more accurate the position it reports to you.

For example, the receiver might read "Distance: 2.8 miles, Bearing: 185°." But just knowing where the cache is located on the planet is only half the battle. It sounds easy, but as you will discover it may take more work than you think. Not only will you have to navigate uncharted terrain, but when you reach the location it may take some serious searching, depending on the accuracy of the GPS receiver (both yours and the hider's) and the craftiness of the hider.

Take Something

Congratulations! You've discovered your first geocache. Now what? Well, let's crack it open and see what you have found.

After pulling off the watertight lid, we find a bunch of items, or *SWAG*, stored in resealable bags. Items are stored in plastic bags to keep them clean, organized, and dry. Let's see: a stress ball, a book on dog training, a couple of silver dollars, and a "Best of the '80s" CD. You have worked hard for it, now choose your reward! You snag the CD for the ride home.

GEO-LINGO

SWAG. Stands for "stuff we all get." It includes the trade items left in caches by geocachers.

Leave Something

If you do take something, don't forget to replace the item with something else for the next lucky visitor to discover. The treasure can be almost anything you might feel is valuable, but try to replace the item you found with something of equal or greater value. Because you planned ahead, you assembled your own swag in a plastic bag to leave behind. Placing a cool key chain that includes a compass, a minilight, and a carabiner in the cache, you leave a true treasure for the next person to find.

Sign the Logbook

The geocache's logbook is the physical record of your visit. Record the date of your visit and any items you took or left. It's there to record not only your presence, but your experiences as well. Feel free to include details about your adventure, the weather, and any interesting sights along the way. When the logbook gets full and the geocache owner swaps it out for a new one, he will have a souvenir for his own efforts of hiding the cache.

Often the owner will leave a disposable camera. Take a picture of yourself and your group. The cache's owner will enjoy seeing who showed up at the cache. Who knows? Maybe your picture will be posted on a website and seen by people all over the world!

Cache In Trash Out

On your geocaching adventure, don't forget to give back to the outdoors and leave the area a little cleaner than you found it. Cache In Trash Out (CITO) is an ongoing environmental initiative adopted by geocachers to encourage good outdoor civic responsibility. While out geocaching, carry a trash bag to pack out whatever trash you find along the trail. Doing so not only sets a good example for other hikers, it also improves the natural beauty of the area.

Share Your Experience Online

After you return to the warmth and safety of your keyboard, you also have an opportunity to share your experience with others online. Make sure to return to the geocaching website and post a log entry for the geocache listing, which informs the online community of your find. If you have any digital photos of the experience, you can upload them for others to view. Just be careful to avoid giving away too much information in the online logs so others have the same challenge locating the cache.

This is also a great time to inform the owner of the geocache if there are any issues with the placement. Is there construction going on in the area? Is the placement of the cache appropriate? Is there a leak in the container? Is the logbook full and in need of replacement? Any feedback that can help update the geocache owner on the cache's status is always welcome.

EUREKA!

When writing your online log it's good to remember "The Four T's":

Trip—Tell a little about your adventure. What did you see, what was the day like?

Traps—Did you encounter any difficulties that might be important to pass on to other geocachers?

Trades—What did you take? What did you leave? Were there any Travel Bugs or other trackable items in the geocache?

Thanks—Just like your mom taught you. Say "thanks" to the geocache owner for the experience!

Learn the Language

Over the years, geocaching has developed its own set of terms, slang, and abbreviations. If you play the game for any length of time, terms like *muggle* and **FTF** will become a natural part of your vocabulary.

You can check out the glossary for a more complete list of caching and navigational terms, but here is a quick rundown of the most common geocaching slang:

- **BYOP.** An acronym for "bring your own pen/pencil," which is often used by cache owners to communicate to other geocachers that you will need to bring your writing utensil in order to sign the cache logbook.

- **FTF.** "First to find"—the first person to log a particular geocache as found. Sometimes there are FTF prizes left in the cache by the owner for this person. These are special items and do not require equal trade.

- **Geocoin.** A small minted coin with "Track at Geocaching. com" on one side and a customized impression on the other. Like Travel Bugs, they can be tracked through Geocaching. com.

- **Muggle.** A nongeocacher. Someone who is not in on the big secret that there are treasures hidden all around them; based on the term "Muggle" from the *Harry Potter* series, which is a nonmagical person.

- **Spoiler.** Information in a geocache log that gives away too many details of a cache location, spoiling the experience for the next geocachers who want to find it. Also used to describe a person who gives away details to other geocachers.

- **SWAG.** Stands for "stuff we all get." It includes the trade items left in caches by geocachers.

- **TFTC.** Geocaching shorthand for "thanks for the cache."

- **TNLN.** Stands for "took nothing left nothing." Usually written in cache logbooks by geocachers who do not trade for material contents in a cache.

- **Travel Bug.** A trackable tag that you attach to an item. The item becomes a hitchhiker that is carried from cache to cache (or person to person) in the real world. You can follow its progress online at Geocaching.com.

- **Waypoint.** A selected point-of-interest location that can be saved, stored, and recalled from a GPS receiver's memory. Cache locations are saved as waypoints.

Log On Before Heading Out

Now you know how the game is played, and you even know a little of the language, but before you head outdoors you'll first need to go online and find a cache in your area.

Geocaching.com is the original and primary international site for geocachers. It includes an extensive list of caches throughout the United States and almost every other country around the world. The website includes a great deal of information on how to get started and how to search for caches, and explanations about what GPS is and how it works. This site also has chat forums and useful links. Surfing around the website is a great way to get up to speed on the activity.

From the website, you can also find links to regional groups and organizations for nearly every state or major area. Many of these groups have websites full of informative local information. Many groups sponsor events, camping, pizza nights, and tournaments that make it easy to get involved and keep in touch with fellow geocachers in your area.

Trinkets Can Be Treasures

There are many rewards when geocaching, and everyone has her own personal favorites. Some thrive on the adventure and excitement of discovery. Others enjoy arriving at a destination they wouldn't have otherwise visited. But many, especially kids, are in it for the treasure.

You're not going to get rich from this treasure, but you're bound to find some unique items along the way. Caches are filled with just about anything that someone might find of value, whether you think so or not! From dollar store finds to handmade items, a cornucopia of unusual treasure is waiting to be found.

For your own personal trade items, use your imagination and have fun. Consider the items you leave as a reflection of yourself. Items don't need to be expensive, but unique prizes that will delight the next finder.

A List of Favorites

Let's be creative and resourceful to raise the bar on cache prizes. "Just use common sense and you should never have to apologize for what you left," says geocacher Jolly B. Good. Here are some examples of good swag:

- Baseball cards
- Batteries (known by cachers as "GPS food")
- Books
- Buttons
- Camping gear
  - Carabiners
  - Compass
  - Emergency blanket
  - Hand and foot warmers
  - Maps
  - Rain ponchos
  - Small flashlights or LED lights
  - Whistle
- Calculators
- Collector's items

- Disposable cameras (but do not take the cache's)
- Dollar store items
- CDs, DVDs, or videos
- Flags
- Gemstones
- Gift certificates
- Geocaching website gear (stickers, hats, pins)
- Money (cash, coins, or silver dollars)
- Small first-aid kits
- Stickers
- Tools (small items such as tape measures)
- Toys
  - Action figures
  - Crayons or colored chalk
  - Decks of cards
  - Die-cast cars and trucks
  - Puzzles
  - Games

Geocacher Signature Items

The Lone Ranger had his silver bullets, Kilroy knew how to tell everyone he had been here, and—in the same vein—geocachers have *signature items*.

GEO-LINGO

A **signature item** is a trademark item used as a geocacher's calling card. These are often custom cards, tags, stickers, or geocoins bearing the geocacher's name and often a favorite phrase or graphic to sum up the geocacher's philosophy.

Signature items grew out of a desire to leave more than just a name in the logbook—to provide something tangible and personal for other geocachers. A signature item might be nothing more than a personalized business card with the geocacher's contact information and a design, or it might be an elaborate homemade item that shows off his own creativity.

Many of these signature items become collector items for other geocachers. Finding a local geocacher's geocoin in a cache can sometimes feel like owning a Babe Ruth rookie card.

If you want to create your own signature item, think of something that reflects your own interests. If you're into snowboarding, you could design a stamp with a snowboarder and your username. If you like spiders, create a spider out of wire and attach it to a piece of cardboard with your name. You don't have to spend a lot of money to create a unique item to leave in caches. And other geocachers can get to know you by the items you leave for them.

Prohibited Geocache Items

Geocachers do their best to self-regulate their sport to keep the activity in a positive light. However, as with any activity, there can always be the occasional bad egg. Because this is a family activity, not only should we obey the local laws, we also need to apply common sense to the items placed in a cache. Even so, some items that may seem harmless can be inappropriate cache items. The following are examples of inappropriate cache items:

- Alcohol
- Ammunition, knives, explosives, or weapons
- Drugs or drug paraphernalia
- Food
- Pornography

Food? We list food because animals can find food even faster than the best geocachers. Animals have been known to chew through caches to get to food and other items that smell, including wrapped candy and chapstick.

An additional consideration when leaving items in a geocache is weather and seasonal changes. Liquid bubbles might seem like a great idea in the summer, but come winter they can freeze and break their bottles. Crayons might seem great in the winter, but during the summer they can liquefy in a hot ammo can and ruin the contents of the cache.

Areas Where Geocaches Are Found

Geoaches can be found almost anywhere, from remote mountain peaks, to city parks, to dense urban jungles. This is the beauty of the game: It can be played anywhere. You can discover caches in a park next to your neighborhood, in another city while on vacation, or in many exotic locations around the world. Here are some advantages to caching in these different environments.

Wide-Open Spaces

What makes geocaching truly special is that it will take you to beautifully scenic areas you would probably never take the time to seek out for yourself. We all enjoy a scenic drive in the country, but how often do we push ourselves to climb up and over that next ridge? Geocaching might involve a trip to a waterfall just off the beaten path, rock climbing, or a multiday hike. It is also not uncommon to hear, "Wow, this place is great, I never knew it existed!" Enjoy the discovery of new places and try to return to share the location with your loved ones.

Parks

Okay, so you don't always have time to take a day or two off work and pack up all your gear to venture off into the great unknown. In our fast-paced lives, parks are great places to take a breather and relax with the family or fun places to picnic and play with the kids on the playground. They are close to home and easily accessible. Because neighborhood parks are not far, even an hour spent in one feels like a rewarding outing. What's even better is that many of these areas include a cache or two. Park caches are typically easy to find, allowing kids of all ages to help take part in the search. These types of areas also enable people to go geocaching on their lunch hours!

> **NAVIGATIONAL NUGGETS**
>
> Outdoor navigation and travel is much easier if you are organized. Keep all of your essential gear in a bag or pack. This saves time and helps to ensure you will not forget anything.

CurmudgeonlyGal reaches in for the find.
(Michelle Davison)

Urban Jungles

A good percentage of our world is made up of concrete and steel. Skyscrapers replace mountains, and wildlife tends to be of the two-legged variety. Don't let that stop you from taking part in geocaching adventures. Geocaches are hidden in all parts of cities. Micro caches are often used to make them easier to hide. Statues and landmarks may also serve as virtual caches. Remember: Do not let your location discourage you. Caches can be found nearly anywhere you may live or go.

Pack Your Pack

Finally! You are almost ready to go. You are so close to finding your first cache you can almost feel those elusive prizes in your hand! Not quite yet: First things first. It's time to pack our bags before heading out. You may have your GPS receiver ready, but there is a bit of planning to go before hitting the trail.

Being prepared with all the right gear can help get you where you want to be.
(Brian Sniatkowski)

We recommend setting up a bag, waist pack, or small day pack with all the basics neatly organized and always ready to go. This way, when the phone rings and it is time to go play, you do not have to search the house, garage, and car for all of your stuff.

Here is the basic list of gear to take with you:

- **GPS receiver.** Don't forget the power cord so you can use it in the vehicle on the way there.

- **Batteries.** Bring a lot of AA's. Not only are they necessary food for your GPS receiver, they are also good to have for your flashlight or camera.

- **Maps.** Bring general maps of the roadways to get there, and a more detailed topographic map of the area. Waterproof map cases with marking pens are also helpful.

- **Flashlight.** It can get dark when venturing into the unknown.

- **Compass.** Get one with a dial-in declination adjustment.

- **Notepad and pen.** Keep them in a watertight bag.

- **Geocache repair kit.** It's always good to bring some items to help repair caches you find on your trip. Extra pens, log-books, sealable sandwich bags, and duct tape are good to repair leaks, protect contents, and replace missing items.

Going Out a Little Farther?

It is not so much survival of the fittest as it is survival of the smartest. If you are going anywhere off the beaten path, there is always a chance of getting lost, being caught in a storm, or, for whatever reason, getting stranded. We recommend you bring the ten essentials:

1. Water

2. Map and compass

3. Flashlight/batteries/bulb

4. Knife/multitool

5. First-aid kit

6. Extra clothing

7. Matches/fire starter

8. Sunscreen/sunglasses

9. Signal mirror

10. Whistle

NAVIGATIONAL NUGGETS

If you do remote wilderness travel, consider using a PLB, a personal locator beacon. Now available in the United States, these transmitters broadcast a satellite-based emergency beacon to allow rescuers to find your exact location anywhere in the world.

Be sure to pack your special medications such as insulin for diabetics or prescription eyewear. In any outdoor situation, the best food and water is what you bring with you. Take a little extra of both: Someone else will forget, and you are covered in the event you extend your stay a little longer than expected. Drinking untreated water and eating from nature's salad bar will not provide the calories needed for outdoor activities, and will most likely make you sick.

Be sure to tell someone where you are going. In your car, leave an extra copy of the geocache's information page, including the coordinates, or write this information on a travel itinerary—we provide one in the back of this book. Taking the time to do so will pay off big if you have a problem. By taking these precautions, search and rescue crews can provide assistance within hours instead of days.

DEAD BATTERIES

Hypothermia is one of the biggest threats to outdoor enthusiasts. It is easy to get caught in a storm, but improper clothing will result in getting soaked through, resulting in the rapid loss of body heat. Most cases of hypothermia occur between 30 and 50 degrees Fahrenheit. Keeping dry will go a long way to improve your comfort and survivability.

Dress for Success

There is no bad weather, only inappropriate gear. Just as with packing gear and supplies, extra clothing is better than not enough. In hot or cold climates, it is typically best to cover up with long-sleeve shirts and pants. This protects the skin from scratches, insect bites, and sunburn. Wear clothing and a jacket that will shed water; your apparel should be made of fabrics that wick moisture away from your body. Also, wear layers you can remove to prevent overheating. Cotton clothing, such as T-shirts and jeans, absorb water and perspiration, sometimes taking days to dry. If you get wet and cold, it is difficult to regain heat, which increases the risk of hypothermia.

Garmin Rino 530HCx GPS receiver with FRS and GMRS radio
and peer-to-peer tracking
(Image used courtesy of Garmin Ltd. or its affiliates.
Copyright © Garmin Ltd. or its affiliates.)

Don't forget a hat! Wide-brimmed boonie-style hats work great. They provide good cover from the rain and sun. Baseball caps leave the back of your neck exposed. Also, wear a good pair of boots that provide ankle support, and keep an extra pair of socks in your gear bag. Is all of this really important? Not if you're visiting a park for an hour or two, but it is in any wilderness environment. We want you to enjoy your outdoor geocaching experience, not be miserable because you're unprepared.

Geocacher Communication

Can you hear me now? If not, try the right frequency. Yes, geocachers use their own radio frequencies on the FRS (Family Radio Service) band in North America and the PMR (Private Mobile Radio) band in Europe. These bands are used in walkie-talkies, which are reasonably inexpensive and do not require a license to operate. The range is limited, however, often to a mile or less depending upon the terrain. On FRS, the geocaching community uses channel 2 with channel 12 as an alternative. On the PMR band, use channel 2 with channel 8 as the alternative. And for those who are into ham radio, the standard geocaching frequency is 147.555.

Garmin International makes a series of GPS receivers that include FRS and GMRS (General Mobile Radio Service) radio frequencies. These receivers are unique in that they work as GPS receivers and two-way walkie-talkies, and have a tracking feature that allows others within range using the same model of unit to appear on the screen. This peer-to-peer tracking is a great way to keep track of the group as well as stay in radio communication.

The Least You Need to Know

- When you find a geocache, take something, leave something, and sign the logbook. Don't forget to share your experience online.
- Visit Geocaching.com to find geocache listings in your area.
- Geocaches are hidden in all types of outdoor environments.
- The success of your outdoor experience will greatly improve with the right gear and clothing.

How GPS Works

In This Chapter

- Understand what GPS is and how it works
- Discover how accurate the gear can be
- Learn what satellite reception is needed for accurate navigation
- Find out about the limitations of GPS technology, and why it does not replace the map and compass

Letterboxers have been hiding containers in the moors of England using hints and puzzles to guide people to their locations for over 100 years. Ham radio operators cleverly hide radio transmitters and search for them using the technology they've come to know and love. In many ways, geocaching is the latest incarnation of that age-old game of hide-and-seek, making use of the latest technology available.

In this chapter, you'll learn about the origins of the Global Positioning System (GPS) and how it works. You'll get a good understanding of how accurate the gear can be, as well as how to check and improve accuracy to make sure you're on track. After getting to know GPS, you'll understand why it doesn't completely replace traditional navigational methods like the map and compass.

In 1957 all eyes were on space. The Soviet Union had trumped the United States by launching the world's first artificial satellite—

Sputnik. The world watched the night skies hoping for a glimpse of this modern marvel as it traveled in its orbit.

Scientists noticed that Sputnik's relative position in space could be calculated based on the length of the radio waves received from it. A theory was developed at Johns Hopkins University's Applied Physics Laboratory based on these observations and submitted as part of a proposal to the Navy Bureau of Ordinance. The proposal became Transit, the precursor to the Global Positioning System.

The U.S. government, with an investment of billions of dollars, developed GPS. Now anyone with an investment in a GPS receiver can use it. Like cell phones and Hummers, this is military technology that we civilians have adopted for uses both practical and fun, like geocaching. Read on to learn everything you wanted to know but were afraid to ask about GPS.

Evolution of the GPS Receiver

GPS is a gift from the U.S. Department of Defense. It currently is a system of 31 satellites broadcasting special radio signals down to Earth that are intercepted by GPS receivers. The receivers analyze the signals to determine the location of receivers anywhere in the world. There has not been such a quantum leap in navigation since the Chinese invented the compass 800 years ago. Imagine: We now have the ability to record our favorite locations and return to them again. Getting lost has never been so much fun. It sounds too good to be true, but, like anything electronic, there are limitations.

EUREKA!

Contrary to popular belief, GPS satellites are not in geosynchronous orbits. They make 2 orbits around the earth every 24 hours and can be maneuvered into different flight paths.

This is one of the reasons signal coverage may vary from day to day and your readings might be different from those taken on the day the cache was placed.

The origins of GPS began in the 1960s as a concept for a worldwide U.S. military navigational system. By the mid-1970s, it became a joint effort of various branches of the U.S. military and was referred to as Navstar. Despite the official name, GPS is the term that stuck.

The system's first major public debut was in 1991 when it contributed to the overwhelming success in the first Iraqi war, Desert Storm. With the system still in its infancy, only 16 satellites were utilized, with many specifically positioned over the Persian Gulf area. Hand-held receivers, primitive by today's standards, helped Allied forces navigate and maneuver around enemy positions in an unfamiliar, featureless desert. The system was considered fully operational in 1995.

In the late 1990s, improvements were made to allow receivers to track 12 satellites simultaneously, instead of the older single-channel units (which were not quite as accurate and much slower in getting a good satellite fix). Also at this time, the prices for GPS receivers began to drop, which allowed more people access to the technology.

All you need is a GPS and a sense of adventure.
(Martyn Hancock)

Useful Gear for Work and Play

GPS obviously has many applications for the military, engineers, and emergency service agencies, but this was a major development for us technology enthusiasts who love the latest technology gadgets. Even better yet, this is something that is practical enough to actually use. For those of us who enjoy the outdoors, GPS provides us a little more freedom and confidence in backcountry travel with the reduced risk of getting lost.

With the ability to save locations as waypoints and create routes using road maps, this technology has, for the most part, removed the uncertainty and guesswork from navigation. For example, we can plot a course from our home to a geocache and the GPS will choose the best route for us to follow. Once there, we can save the location of a trailhead, venture off in a different direction to explore, and still return to the exact location of any saved waypoint. This could be done with traditional navigational skills through map reading and dead reckoning, but it's not nearly as efficient or fun as using GPS.

Satellite Signals

A GPS receiver is essentially a computer that receives signals broadcast from GPS satellites. That's why a GPS unit is referred to as a receiver, or GPSr. There are currently 31 satellites orbiting around the earth. GPS receivers need to read the signals of at least three satellites at a time to determine the equipment's exact location, a process known as trilateration. Four are needed for a more accurate three-dimensional fix providing elevation and the precise atomic time. The more satellites the receiver can lock on to, the more accurate the position information.

Trilateration works by a receiver downloading radio signals broadcast from each satellite it can lock on to. The GPS receiver calculates its location by determining the distance from each overhead satellite. Satellites broadcast their radio signals in a sphere. The unit's computer determines its location by determining where all of the spheres intercept. This is why accuracy readings substantially increase with the more satellites a receiver can lock on to.

NAVIGATIONAL NUGGETS

GPS devices are known as receivers because they intercept special radio signals broadcast from GPS satellites to determine their location on Earth. There is often confusion over whether someone else can track the user's position. Recreational GPS gear does not transmit data. No one will know your position unless you have communication equipment adequate enough to tell them.

The government broadcasts two sets of coded signals. Military equipment can receive both the (P) and (CA) signals for highly accurate readings. Civilian gear accepts only the slightly less accurate (CA) code. Despite this limitation, most receivers with a clear view of the sky are accurate within 49 feet (15 meters) more than 90 percent of the time.

Features of GPS Receivers

Modern receivers offer many features, maybe more than you'll ever need or use. All of the buttons and screens can be a bit overwhelming. Despite being a high-tech electronic item, they are actually quite easy to use. The more you practice with the gear, the more your intimidation will turn into interest as your confidence grows.

Regardless of the brand, size, or price, GPS receivers are designed to provide the same basic functions. More expensive models provide a greater memory storage capability and provide a basemap to display on the receiver's screen. Even the least expensive models provide many of the following basic features:

- A display indicating your position anywhere in the world, typically within 49 feet (15 meters) of accuracy. The current location is displayed on a view screen as a pointer icon.

- Receivers record data that is displayed on the view screen and stored in the unit's memory. Such data includes saved points of interest known as waypoints, as well as an electronic breadcrumb trail indicating where you have traveled, known as a track log.

- Time of day, elevation, speed, compass readings, and estimated time of arrival.

- A pointer, bearing, distance, and estimated time of arrival to selected waypoint destinations.

- More expensive models provide a built-in basemap. These are electronic maps provided from the manufacturer. For instance, a receiver's basemap may include all of North America or the United Kingdom.

- More expensive receivers provide additional memory for map storage. This is used to enhance the basemap with topographical map data or other information selected by the user, available online or on a CD-ROM from the manufacturer.

NAVIGATIONAL NUGGETS

GPS receivers provide elevation information after acquiring a fix on four or more satellites. This altimeter function is usually not as accurate as the location data, but will most likely get you within 100 feet (27 meters). Some receivers have a built-in barometric altimeter to help ensure greater accuracy.

How Accurate Is Accurate?

Accuracy remains about the same regardless of the brand, size, or price of a receiver. Receivers work on line of sight to the overhead satellites, so the whole trick to accuracy is allowing the antenna to get a clear view of the sky. Because the government's selective availability is no longer in effect, a GPS receiver should be able to lock on to its location anywhere in the world within 49 feet (15 meters) more than 90 percent of the time. Not perfect, but somewhere within 49 feet will be close enough to find a cache, your camp, or anything else you might be looking for.

Thankfully, in May 2000, the government eliminated selective availability. This was a military safeguard that deliberately made the GPS signals civilians could receive inaccurate by 100 yards, or 91 meters.

The government got around the security problem by scrambling the signal around military bases and other sensitive sites. As previously mentioned, this major development allowed caches to be hidden and found again, inspiring the game of geocaching.

Receivers can also provide elevation information. Unfortunately, their altimeter function is not always as accurate as their other location data. Altitude readings may be off as much as 100 yards (91 meters). Special systems have been developed for aviation and boating, for which absolute accuracy is required for autopilot features and for navigating around hazards in low visibility. Accuracy is improved by including radio signal broadcasts that help fine-tune the user's position. There are two systems that increase GPS accuracy, the original differential correction, known as DGPS, and WAAS. The DGPS system is primarily used around seaports and waterways and requires an additional differential beacon receiver.

WAAS

Fortunately, a new system that improves accuracy considerably has been developed. Known as the wide-area augmentation system (WAAS), this system typically improves accuracy from 15 meters down to 3. It was created for the aviation industry and includes 25 ground reference stations with a master station on each U.S. coast. These stations monitor and correct GPS signal interference caused by satellite drift and signal delay through the ionosphere. The corrected messages are then broadcast from one of two geostationary satellites. This corrected signal improves accuracy to less than 3 meters 95 percent of the time. Currently, WAAS is available only in the United States, although other governments in Europe and Asia are developing similar systems.

Most GPS receivers sold after 2000 are capable of accepting WAAS signals. Luckily, there is no additional cost or equipment needed to use this system. When using your receiver, check the satellite status page to determine whether the system is searching for, or has picked up, WAAS signals. Be aware that the WAAS feature uses more battery power. Your receiver can most likely be set to turn this feature off if battery use is an issue.

Factors That Affect Accuracy

The main cause of inaccuracies in civilian GPS equipment is iono-spheric interference. This is caused by the delay of radio waves as they travel through electron fields in the ionosphere. Military receivers send two sets of signals that allow the ionospheric delay to be measured and compensated for. Nothing can be done for civilians to correct this inaccuracy other than DGPS and WAAS. Civilian GPS users must learn to accommodate for the equipment's inaccuracy.

A second problem is multipath interference. This is caused by error from a receiver picking up satellite radio signals that have bounced from terrain obstacles, such as buildings or cliff walls. Civilian receivers cannot distinguish the ricocheting signals from the ones traveling directly from the satellite to the receiver. Water droplets on overhead vegetation can also cause this problem. Be aware of your surroundings and understand that overhead vegetation, especially if it is wet or snow covered, will distort GPS signals considerably.

If you doubt the accuracy of your position, check the satellite status page to determine the current signal strength and quality. You may have to get into a clearing for a better view of the sky. Also be aware that tall buildings and cliff walls are a factor. Sometimes adjusting the receiver itself helps; receivers with built-in antennas work best when held straight up and down.

Getting a Fix

When you fire up the receiver by pressing the power button, the computer begins seeking out satellites. You have a satellite fix when the receiver picks up enough "birds" (satellites) to activate the navigation process. GPS radio signals work on line of sight, meaning they travel to the receiver in a straight line. So we know the signals will not bend around obstacles like heavy tree coverage or cave walls, but fog, dust, rain, or other extreme weather conditions do not affect them.

Depending on the quality of an antenna and a user's position, an average of seven or eight satellites may be locked on at any one time. Under ideal circumstances, such as on a hilltop, all 12 may be received. Only picking up three signals will result in a two-dimensional (2-D) reading. This operation will provide location information that may be inaccurate by as much as several miles, and no elevation data will be provided. At a minimum, four satellites are needed to obtain a three-dimensional (3-D) fix. This will provide reasonably accurate location and elevation data. Accuracy is greatly improved with every additional satellite received.

When in doubt, check the satellite status page on your GPS receiver often to determine what kind of accuracy you can expect. This page provides a great deal of information, including the receiver's working status and the number of signals received at any given time. Through graphs, the signal strength will appear for each satellite. A satellite geometry graph will display how they are positioned overhead. This is important because satellites clumped together or arranged in a straight line provide poor geometry. The best satellite geometry is provided when there is at least one satellite directly overhead, with several others on the surrounding horizon.

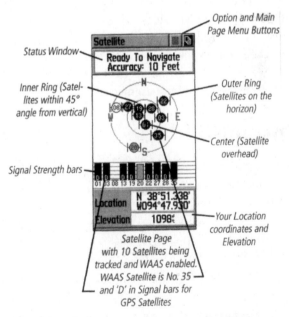

(Image used courtesy of Garmin Ltd. or its affiliates.
Copyright © Garmin Ltd. or its affiliates.)

Two different accuracy readings are also provided. There is a signal strength indicator known as the DOP, or dilution of precision, number. The smaller the DOP number, the better the satellite geometry. Good satellite reception is represented by the number 2 or smaller. Readings below the number 3 should provide accuracy within 15 meters. Readings from 4 to 6 could provide inaccuracies up to 100 meters. A reading of 6 indicates that the receiver is failing to maintain a satellite lock.

The other indicator is the EPE, estimated position error, number. This measurement also considers satellite geometry to determine the estimated accuracy in feet or meters. Check out these readings often to determine your level of accuracy and to ensure the antenna and gear are working properly.

Initialization

When you turn on the receiver for the first time, it will not be sure of its location. The gear needs to initialize itself to determine its location. This process is also necessary if the receiver has traveled a few hundred miles away from its home area with the power shut off, such as when you take it on vacation. The receiver may initialize automatically, although it may be necessary to point out your approximate location on the receiver's basemap.

DEAD BATTERIES

Is it your first time turning on your new GPS? Find an area with lots of open sky, turn your GPS on, and let it sit for about 15 minutes. This gives it time to download the almanac that will tell it where in the sky to look for GPS satellites.

This is also a good thing to do if you've left the GPS turned off and without batteries for a long period of time.

To initialize a receiver, go outside to an area with a clear view of the sky and turn the receiver's power on. The unit may prompt you to select an initializing method. If your receiver includes a basemap, choose By Map. Use the cursor arrow to zoom to your current location on the map page and press Enter. The receiver will now start to read satellites from the new location. After satellites are fixed, the present position pointer icon will appear in the center of the map page to show your exact location. When the receiver switches over the map page showing your position, it is an indication that enough satellites are received for the equipment's navigation function to work properly. Now you're ready to go.

GPS Limitations

Wow, we can know exactly where we are at any time, anywhere in the world. With that kind of technological power, we can toss out the maps and compass and forget about paying attention to where we are going, right? Not exactly. There are still limitations to the Global Positioning System. For one, receivers are electronic just like your cell phone and computer hard drive. You wouldn't trust your life to one of those, would you? Gear can fail. It can also be damaged, lost, water-logged, or stolen.

The other issue is that it needs power to operate. If you have the equipment set up in your vehicle, plugged into the cigarette lighter, it's not a problem; you can leave it on all day. For hiking and geocaching, however, the gear has to rely on battery power. A receiver with dead batteries is nothing more than an expensive doorstop. Check the battery gauge. This meter usually looks like an E-to-F fuel gauge and is often found on the satellite status page. Always carry at least six or more spare AA batteries in a resealable plastic bag. Even if your receiver doesn't run out of power, you may need them for your flashlight or camera.

Even though GPS receivers include a compass feature, they do not replace the traditional compass. This is because the receiver's compass will not work if the gear is in a stationary position. A receiver has to be traveling at least 4 miles per hour before its computer can calculate the direction you are traveling. This is why, when you ask your receiver to navigate to a waypoint, the compass pointer arrow could be off in any direction, which we refer to as "loose bearings." When you start moving, the arrow immediately aligns to the correct bearing.

GPS manufacturers have attempted to get around this problem by adding electronic compasses to receivers. This is a good idea, although they can be a bit cumbersome to use and the feature drains batteries faster. So, you still need a good old-fashioned compass.

As you can see, GPS still cannot completely replace the traditional map and compass. Equipment failure and dead batteries are not that uncommon, and getting lost or stranded turns a pleasurable outing into a serious nightmare. Because the consequences could be tragic, navigational skills are too important not to learn.

Knowing traditional navigational skills will greatly increase your confidence in backcountry travel and allow you to use your GPS receiver to its fullest capacity. Besides, you need to know how to read a map and compass to go geocaching! Part 3 covers using GPS, maps, and a compass in detail.

The Least You Need to Know

- GPS is a U.S. government technology that anyone can use.
- GPS devices calculate their positions by receiving satellite signals.
- GPS receiver accuracy is typically within 15 meters and can be improved further with the aid of WAAS.
- GPS receivers need to lock on a minimum of three satellites to navigate accurately.
- GPS devices have limitations besides their accuracy: they can fail, and their batteries go dead.
- Learning traditional navigational skills helps ensure that you can navigate to a geocache and safely return if your electronic gear should fail.

Get Out and Play

So you've got a basic understanding of how to go out and find a geo-cache, and you understand how GPS works. Now it's time to go out and explore everything geocaching has to offer. You might be sur-prised to learn that there's more to it than just hiking in the woods: city slickers can even geocache without leaving sight of an espresso shop! In this part, you learn about the many geocaching variations. Maybe you'll come up with one of your own!

Are you excited at the thought of finding your first geocache? Great! In Part 2, you'll learn how to find geocaches online before finding them outdoors. We cover everything you need to know to find even the toughest geocaches, and then we discuss how to hide your own. After that, we go over some potential hazards to avoid so that you can safely return from your geocaching adventures in one piece.

In Part 2, you also discover Travel Bugs and other trackable geo-caching items. These items represent their owners, often traveling from geocache to geocache accomplishing goals around the world.

Before You Leave Home

In This Chapter

- Learn how to search for geocaches
- Set up your own user profile
- What to consider before seeking a geocache
- Use maps and aerial photos
- Learn how to submit your own geocache

After learning the basics, at last it's time to go geocaching.

Before we find a geocache outdoors, we first have to identify a geocache to seek online. In this chapter you'll learn the many ways to select a geocache as well as how to get the maps and clues you need to ensure success. Do you use a personal digital assistant (PDA)? We'll show you how to download lists of caches to take with you. You'll also learn about the maps and aerial photos available, and we'll show you how to post a geocache of your own.

As the official global headquarters for geocaching, Geocaching.com provides a great number of resources to support new geocachers. In an ongoing effort to support the worldwide geocaching community, the Geocaching.com site is also under constant development as new technology and user needs come into play. Spend some time cruising around the site and checking out the various features.

Developing Your Geocacher Profile

One of the first steps you can take to get involved in geocaching and become a member of its community is to create your own account. This is your opportunity to provide a geocacher name, e-mail address, the area where you're from, a photo or image, and other details you want to share with the community. Other geocachers will be able to access your profile to learn a little more about you and what geocaches you may have found or hidden. With your new geocache identity, you'll also be able to participate in discussion forums. And remember, you won't be able to see the coordinates for geocaches unless you are logged into your Geocaching.com account. Note: A basic membership on Geocaching.com is free.

Searching for Nearby Geocaches

Searching for nearby geocaches is easy. In fact, they're everywhere! You will be surprised to see the number of listings within 10 miles of where you live. The trick is to know how to select the interesting ones to find. The following is a list of ways to search for the perfect cache to seek:

- **By postal code.** Postal codes are available in the United States as well as several other countries. On the front page of Geocaching.com, simply type in a postal code and click Go. A list of caches will appear in order from the nearest to the farthest from the center of the postal code's region.

- **By state/country.** Select a state or country to search, and then a menu list of cities or states will appear to narrow your search.

- **By keyword.** Search for geocaches by keyword. This method is ideal for recalling caches, especially if you can't remember the entire name.

- **With Google Map.** Geocaching.com provides an amazing set of tools that works in conjunction with Google maps.

Simply enter an address or postal code on Geocaching.com and zoom in or out on the desired area. Switch from map view to satellite, and even check out the terrain and topography maps.

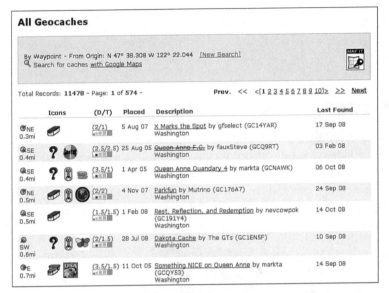

A quick search by postal code provides a long list of geocaches listed by the distance from the postal code's center.

(Geocaching.com)

- **By username.** Search the database for fellow geocachers. Select a username and you can get a list of caches found or hidden by this person.

- **By waypoint name.** When a cache is submitted for posting, the Geocaching.com website creates a unique code for the cache listing. A geocache waypoint begins with "GC" followed by letters and numbers and is seven characters or less so it can fit in the waypoint title field on most GPS receivers.

- **By address.** Based on a physical address, the site determines the approximate coordinates and does a search.

- **By geocache type.** Search for all geocaches or select an individual cache type.

- **By coordinate.** Using a specific waypoint, you can do a distance search from an exact position.

As you can see, there are many ways in which you can search for that perfect cache. All of these features make it easy to get a list of geocaches to find, no matter where you are.

Paperless Geocaching

Geocaching.com provides you with the abilities to download a simple printer-friendly version of cache pages that will save you ink and an Adobe PDF version as well. The PDF version includes the ability to print out hints and the last five or ten logs for a little extra help on the search.

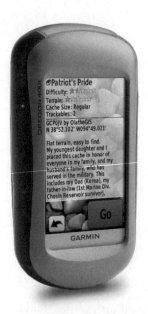

A geocache as it would appear on a Garmin Oregon.

(Image used courtesy of Garmin Ltd. or its affiliates. Copyright © Garmin Ltd. or its affiliates.)

After a few geocaching outings, you'll likely want to switch to something less bulky than paper printouts. You will also soon discover how cumbersome it can be to enter a waypoint for every geocache you want to seek. Hand entering coordinates can sometimes result in accidental errors, perhaps causing your GPS receiver to show a geocache to be 100 feet to 100 miles from its actual location. Double-checking your coordinates before going out on a hunt helps, but fortunately there are alternatives to hand entering coordinates and carrying reams of cache listings along on your geocaching adventures.

As the game has grown, so have the features for both enjoying a paper-free existence and downloading geocache waypoints directly to your GPS unit. With a few simple steps and some free software, you can spontaneously geocache without having to return to your computer.

Downloading Coordinates

Transferring geocache coordinates from the Internet to your GPS receiver is easier than you might think. You need a computer-to-GPS data cable. These cables are available for most brands and models of GPS receivers, with the possible exception of some lower end GPS units. Some more expensive models even come with their own data cable.

After you have a cable, you need to get a file of caches you want to download to your GPS unit. Geocaching.com gives you several options on how to do this. On the page of results, you'll notice there is a check box to the right of every cache listing. Select the caches you want to download to your GPS by checking the box next to each listing, and then click the Download Waypoints button at the bottom of the page.

If you haven't agreed to the data license agreement, you will be redirected to another page. Otherwise your browser will prompt you to save a file named geocaching.loc to your computer. The LOC file format contains a list of coordinates for each selected cache, a web link for the location of each cache description, the names of the caches, and the waypoint names to be downloaded into your GPS unit. Now that you have your waypoint file, you need a software application to open the file and upload the waypoint information to your GPS receiver. Fortunately, many GPS applications support the LOC file format. A list is always available at www.geocaching.com/waypoints.

The software application will ask you to choose your GPS receiver before uploading your cache list, because different units have distinct ways of downloading information. Now all you need to do is send the waypoints to your GPS receiver.

Coordinates on your receiver show each geocache with a name that starts with GC, for geocache. You can use this waypoint name to look up the details about each geocache on the Geocaching.com website. If you prefer, you can change the name of each cache to something more descriptive before uploading it to your unit.

In addition to these features, if you have opted to become a premium member of Geocaching.com, you will also find the option to download individual .gpx files on each cache page. In addition, if you have a Garmin GPS, there is an optional plug-in that allows you to download coordinates directly to your GPS one cache at a time. There's also an option for transferring coordinates to a registered GPS-enabled phone.

> **NAVIGATIONAL NUGGETS**
>
> GPX (GPS eXchange format) files contain a great deal of information beyond just the coordinates for the cache. They also contain the information found on the cache pages and can also include additional waypoints—that is, additional coordinates for parking, trailheads, and other locations pertinent to the geocache.

Pocket Queries

If you own a PDA, such as a Palm or Pocket PC, Pocket Queries can be your best geocaching companion. Pocket Queries is a feature provided for premium members of Geocaching.com. It allows you to receive a file that contains a listing of caches tailored to your interests. You will also be provided a LOC file of the same cache listings to upload to your GPS unit. Using the search feature in many of the GPX file software programs, you can quickly view each cache listing and hints.

Pocket Queries can be customized to search by cache type, caches you haven't found, caches hidden between dates, and many other alternative searches. It's like having a copy of Geocaching.com in your pocket. Up to five queries can be scheduled to generate on a daily basis, and are e-mailed directly to you.

Pocket Queries contain a lot of information. It's always a good idea to click the button at the bottom of the page to have the file compressed into a .zip format. These files are smaller and handled better by e-mail servers.

Check out Chapter 12 for more information about using PDAs and computers with GPS.

Selecting a Geocache to Seek

As you can see, it is quite easy to find geocaches to seek. However, it may be challenging to select one from all that are available. So you found a cache that looks interesting? Let's take a closer look to see whether this might be the one to find first. You need to consider a number of things before packing up the crew and hitting the road.

- **Access.** Is the location next to a parking lot? Is it permissible to use bikes or wheelchairs?

- **Children.** Is the geocache location kid-friendly? Can geocachers bring a stroller, and is there a restroom or a playground nearby?

- **Cost.** Some parks charge for admission.

- **Distance.** Check out the distance so that you can plan how to best get there. Remember, GPS receivers return results as the crow flies (in a straight line) and it is up to you to determine the best navigational route.

- **Dog-friendly.** Check out any factors that might affect whether Rover can come along.

- **Special equipment.** Does the cache location require a special vehicle or other equipment to reach? Some more complex caches may require rock climbing or scuba gear.

- **Terrain.** Get an idea about how far this cache might be off the beaten path. Should you wear shorts and sandals or long pants with boots? Depending on the location, there could be hazards like poison oak or sticker weeds. Remember that for hiking in brushy areas, more clothing coverage is best.

- **Time consideration.** Is this a cache you can snag on your lunch hour or is it a weekend excursion? Travel time will be a factor in determining how long it will take. Be sure to add a little more time than you think you might need.

- **Weather.** Caches in higher elevations could be snowed in for much of the year.

Many of these factors can be found listed as cache attributes on the geocache detail page. These handy little attribute icons help you filter out conditions you would rather not tackle (like poisonous plants or difficult climbs) or filter in conditions you prefer (like caches that are available 24/7 or are in pet-friendly areas).

Cache Difficulty Ratings

Geocaches are rated in two categories, each designated on a five-point scale. Difficulty relates to the mental challenge of finding a cache and terrain describes the physical environment. A 1/1 difficulty/terrain rating would the easiest cache to find, while a 5/5 difficulty/terrain rating would be the most difficult.

When you're ready to post your own geocache, you can fill out the online form through a link on the Resources page on Geocaching. com. There, you can provide additional information about the geocache location, including cache ratings.

Difficulty

★   **Easy.** The geocache is in plain sight or can be found in a few minutes of searching.

★★   **Average.** The average geocacher will be able to find this in less than 30 minutes of searching.

★★★   **Challenging.** An experienced geocacher will find this challenging, and it could take up a good portion of an afternoon.

★★★★   **Difficult.** A real challenge for the experienced geocacher. May require special skills or knowledge, or in-depth preparation to find. May require multiple days or trips to complete.

★★★★★   **Extreme.** A serious mental or physical challenge. Requires specialized knowledge, skills, or equipment to find the geocache.

EUREKA!

Cone_Z (GCKM8M) is a five-star difficulty and five-star terrain cache hidden in Antarctica. The site is 12,000 feet in altitude approximately 7 miles from the ocean (when the ice melts out). If you're interested in going for it you'll have to be one of the few technicians or research team members that visit this very remote and very cold location.

Terrain

★   **Handicapped accessible.** Terrain is likely to be paved, is relatively flat, and requires less than a half-mile hike.

★★   **Suitable for small children.** Terrain is generally along marked trails, and there are no steep elevation changes or heavy overgrowth. Less than a 2-mile hike is required.

★★★   **Not suitable for small children.** The average adult or older child should be okay depending on physical condition. Terrain is likely off-trail. It may have one or more of the following: some overgrowth, some steep elevation changes, or more than a 2-mile hike.

★★★★   **Experienced outdoor enthusiasts only.** Terrain is probably off-trail. It will have one or more of the following: very heavy overgrowth, very steep elevation (requiring use of hands), or more than a 10-mile hike. It may require an overnight stay.

★★★★★   **Requires specialized equipment, knowledge, or experience.** This geocache may require a boat, a four-wheel-drive truck, rock climbing, or scuba gear, or is otherwise extremely difficult.

Using Maps and Clues

So you found a cache to seek out that fits your criteria. The distance, accessibility, and difficulty rating are just right. It's time to take a closer look at the cache's page for clues. There are descriptions offered that will probably provide useful information to its whereabouts. Clues might include details of the area and local landmarks. There might also be comments on what you need to bring along and what the cache itself looks like.

The geocache owner's hint will most likely be encrypted. To read the hint when in the field, you will have to decode it using a letter key system that is provided on the cache's web page. To make it even easier, you can click the Decrypt link to have the hint unscrambled before you set out for your adventure. Remember, this hint will probably tell you where the cache is hidden, so you may not want to decrypt it unless you really have to.

The cache details page includes the option to view the cache using a variety of maps. Street maps can help you select the most efficient route to begin your search. Topographic maps provide you information on the surrounding area—hills, valleys, rivers, and other information that can affect how you approach the cache.

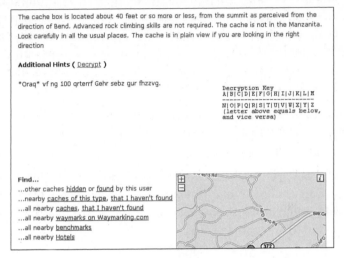

Note the hints that can be provided on a geocache details page.
(Geocaching.com)

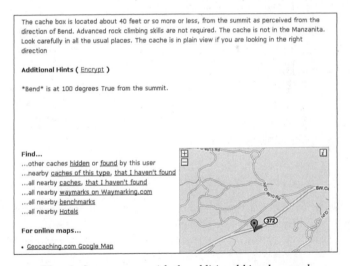

Here is the same page with the additional hint decrypted.
(Geocaching.com)

One of the most useful tools available to you is the Geocaching. com Google Map. This is a fairly new feature that combines the convenience of Google Maps with the details of Geocaching.com. As with all Google Maps, you can zoom in and out; drag the map to a new area; and switch between map view, satellite view, terrain view, and MyTopo. In addition, Geocaching.com provides you with tools to filter various cache types, including those caches you've already found or caches you have hidden.

These maps also include the ability to click on a cache icon to get more detail about that specific geocache type or go directly to the cache page itself.

As with Pocket Queries, access to some of these maps is limited to Geocaching.com premium memberships. Working with these tools will help you realize just how beneficial they can be, but they are not required in order to find geocaches.

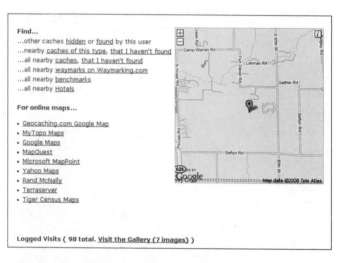

The Google map provided on a Geocaching.com cache details page provides general information about the landscape and area around the geocache.

(Geocaching.com)

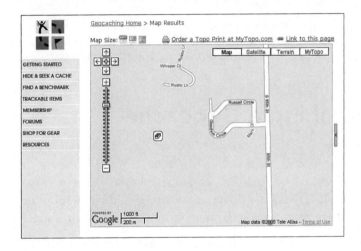

*This is the same map zoomed in using the Google map on Geocaching.com.
Notice that you can also switch to satellite or terrain maps for more information.*
(Geocaching.com)

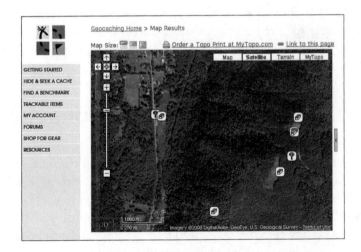

This is an example of a Google map on Geocaching.com in satellite view.
(Geocaching.com)

> **NAVIGATIONAL NUGGETS**
>
> Maps are an essential guide, but don't be surprised if the map does not exactly match the ground. Maps are sometimes inaccurate due to changes over time to roads, trails, waterways, and other features.

Watching a Geocache

Would you like to be notified whenever there is a change to a cache listing, or when a cache is found by another player? Perhaps the cache is in a unique location, or you simply want to be notified when the first finder logs it. Whatever your reason, if you want to be notified of changes to a cache listing you can add it to your watch list.

A watch list is a free feature on Geocaching.com that notifies you via e-mail whenever the status of a chosen cache has changed. When you are logged in, this option is visible for you to select on each cache listing. If you add a listing to your watch list, you can remove it at any time from your account preferences.

Keep in mind that if it is a popular geocache, you may receive a lot of e-mails. Also, there is no need for you to watch your own cache listings because you are automatically notified of changes. Sometimes you can tell the popularity of the cache listing by the number of geocachers who watch it.

Submitting Your Own Geocache

Once you've played the game for a while you'll realize that you know of unique or interesting locations that are important to you that you would like to share with other geocachers. The first step in posting a geocache is to read the Geocache Listing Requirements on Geocaching.com. The guidelines help you in determining all of the information and resources you need in order for a cache to be published. There are a number of do's and don'ts that we will get into in greater detail in the next chapter when we prepare to hide our first geocache.

Some of the features required when posting your own geocache include:

- **Type, size, and name of geocache**
- **Location of geocache and the date placed**
- **Latitude/longitude coordinates in decimal minutes**
- **Overall difficulty and terrain ratings**
- **Short description.** Provide information about the location, including difficulty, terrain, and access.
- **Long description.** Provide details about the cache, including cache contents, what the container looks like, and the relevancy of the location. Is there additional educational or historical information you want to share?
- **Hints/spoiler info.** Hints will be encrypted on the site until a geocacher clicks a link to decrypt it, or decodes it on the trail. Keep your hints short so that decoding it on the trail is easier.
- **Attributes.** These are a series of icons that provide helpful information to geocachers who wish to find specific types of caches. These icons represent unique cache characteristics, including size, whether the cache is kid friendly, if it is available 24 hours a day, if you need special equipment, and more.
- **Travel Bugs.** Want to place a Travel Bug in your geocache? You need to add a log entry to your cache page in order for the Travel Bug to appear in the online inventory of the cache.

After you have compiled all of the information for your geocache, select the Hide and Seek a Cache button on the front page of Geocaching.com, and then click the Cache Submission Form button. Once you have completed all of the required information in the form, click the Report New Listing button.

After reporting your geocache listing, the cache is sent to the volunteer geocacher reviewer community, who reviews the cache submission to make sure that it meets the guidelines for geocache publication. Note that the reviewers do not physically review your cache, they simply review the submitted listing. This process can take a few days, but once it has been reviewed, it is either published, or you are contacted by the reviewer with questions or concerns regarding the cache listing. After your geocache is published, you receive an e-mail confirmation letting you know that the cache is available online. Thereafter, you receive e-mails every time someone logs your geocache.

Disabled Caches

After a geocache is published, the geocache owner is responsible for updating the cache listing about any changes to the cache so that other geocachers are aware of its status. Whether a cache is temporarily disabled for maintenance, has gone missing, or is no longer being managed, it is important to provide up-to-date information to avoid geocachers from looking for a cache that cannot be found. Geocaching.com shows a cache is disabled by placing a line through the title. This means the cache is currently inactive. It can be made active again if the owner reinstates it or agrees to allow someone else to adopt it.

Geocaching websites rely on player feedback to keep the status of caches updated. If you discover a cache is missing, be sure to log on to the website to let the owner know the cache was not found. A cache owner should check out the location if there are an unusual number of Did Not Find log entries. The geocache can be temporarily disabled to allow the owner time to check on it. If a cache owner cannot be contacted, the cache can be adopted or removed completely from the site. If the cache remains disabled or abandoned, it will be archived and removed from the search list altogether.

Posting Photos

Posting photos is a great way to share your geocaching adventures. As the owner of a cache listing or log entry, you have the ability to upload digital photos. Geocachers enjoy viewing the galleries of cache listings, often learning stories of participants from all over the world.

As the cache owner, you may want to provide photo clues to help users find the hiding spot for your cache. Some cache owners show pictures of the general cache location, or a nice photo of the nearby area to entice players to seek out her cache. Some owners even develop and upload photos from disposable cameras left in their caches, which is often informative and, even more often, humorous.

The Least You Need to Know

- Setting up a user profile allows you to join the Geocaching.com community and access geocache coordinates.
- Geocache data can be downloaded into your GPS receiver and PDA.
- Consider the geocache ratings and attributes before seeking a geocache.
- Maps and aerial photos help you analyze the terrain to determine the best way to navigate to a location.

Playing the Game

In This Chapter

- Get ready, it's time to play!
- Hitting the trail to find a geocache
- Learn how to hide a geocache of your own
- Find out how to maintain your geocache
- Learn how to avoid potential problems

In this chapter you'll learn how to go outside and find a geocache or two. After you get that down, its time to learn how to hide and maintain a geocache of your own!

Get Out and Play

At last you've selected a geocache to find. You have a GPS receiver and other gear neatly organized in a pack, and everyone is anxiously waiting to go. But wait, you still have some homework to do. Actually, finding a cache is a little like detective work, a case that needs to be solved. After you select a cache, the sleuthing begins. First some research, as you comb the information page for clues. Then some CIA-type analysis, as you study maps and decrypt secret codes. Finally, it's time for gumshoeing as you seek to solve the mystery of the uniquely hidden geocache you've chosen.

Proper preparation will ensure a fun family geocaching adventure.
(Shane Buckner)

Coordinate Entry

The first step is to enter the geocache coordinates into your GPS receiver. This requires knowing how to save a waypoint. If you do not know how to do this, check out Chapter 10, which covers waypoints in detail.

The standard geographic coordinate system used for geocaching is latitude and longitude. Latitude is a measurement of distance north or south of the equator. Longitude is a measurement of distance east or west of the prime meridian. (The prime meridian is located at Greenwich, England.) Latitude and longitude lines are measured using degrees, minutes, and seconds. More specifically in geocaching, the standard coordinate type is decimal minutes. This means that coordinates are displayed using degrees and decimal minutes instead of a full address of degrees, minutes, and seconds. If this makes no sense to you yet, don't panic! Chapter 11 covers this information in more detail.

A confusing issue with using latitude/longitude coordinates is that they can be displayed in two different formats. The full address includes degrees, minutes, and seconds; or, the seconds are removed and the minutes are converted to a decimal number. On Geocaching.com, the standard coordinate format is decimal minutes.

On the GPS Setup menu, typically under Position, the option usually appears as hddd°.mm.mmm. Also be sure that the map *datum* is in the WGS 84 format in North America. On the same Setup Position screen, the option will appear as [WGS 84]. If you are not in North America, be sure to follow the instructions on the geocache website to set your receiver to whatever datum is used for your part of the world.

 GEO-LINGO

A map **datum** is a global survey system that is used to create maps. Each datum may take a slightly different measurement of the earth. Using the wrong datum can result in positions being off by as much as a mile. The most used datum for geocaching is WGS 84, but many older maps use NAD 27.

Sample set-up menu as shown on a Garmin Colorado GPS.
(Image used courtesy of Garmin Ltd. or its affiliates. Copyright © Garmin Ltd. or its affiliates.)

Okay, so you have the coordinates entered as a waypoint in deci-mal minutes. The waypoint default number has been changed to a six-digit name that references the cache's title. Print out the cache information page to take along. Use it first to double-check the coordinates to ensure every number is absolutely the same as listed on the sheet. Any data-entry error will give you an address possibly hundreds of miles off.

DEAD BATTERIES

Be sure to double-check the coordinates when entering the data into the GPS receiver. Getting one number wrong could result in being 100 miles from the actual cache location. Don't put yourself through the frustration of searching in the wrong area.

Maps and Clues

Many times the cache owner will provide you with good informa-tion about the surrounding area of the cache, possibly even about the container itself. While this is helpful, the cache details page may also contain clues, the main hint being encrypted by the cache owner. You could decrypt the hint now, or make it more challenging by waiting until you have trouble finding the cache. For your first find, however, you should strongly consider decrypting the hint before heading outdoors. Also, if the cache owner does not provide a help-ful cache description, take the time to read recent logs and try to determine what kind of cache container is used. You want your first caching experience to be a positive one, so you might as well arm yourself with as much information as possible to ensure success.

Next, check out the many map links on the page and the map shown for the listing. It will be a general map, possibly showing the cache's location in reference to the nearest town or city. Geocaching.com provides you with links to various online map sites, some of which may provide you with turn-by-turn directions to the general area of the cache.

Reviewing the map is important because you have to find the cache area before getting out and actually finding the cache. Often there is more than one way to access the area. A little analysis may be required to figure out the best route to take. The road that gets you closest to the cache may not leave you at the best route to take when you get off the road.

When you know the general area where the cache is located, it's time to check out the topographic maps. They give greater detail of terrain features through the use of contour lines. Based on the location and potential difficulty, you can decide whether you need to buy an additional detailed topographic map.

Remember, even if your GPS receiver includes routing maps, getting to the actual geocache location can sometimes be difficult. There could be obstacles that lie between you and that elusive geocache. Waterways, mountains, cliffs, or simply no trail are all examples of potential challenges. Another consideration is the access road itself. A map's collar information should reveal the type of roadway going in. The collar is the section across the bottom of a map that contains the map's reference information. That way you'll know whether you can travel in a Honda Civic or a Land Rover.

Finally, review the geocache details page and make sure that the cache owner has not already provided additional waypoints for the cache you are seeking. These waypoints might include information about the best parking location or trailhead near the geocache. Very often you will find it easier to navigate to these locations with this additional information.

Road Trip!

The maps are printed and the gang is confident we know where we're going. It's time to fire up the GPS. After we get a satellite fix, we ask the receiver to show us the way to the geocache waypoint. Within a moment, the data is revealed. Distance is 21.8 miles at a bearing of 86° east. That doesn't sound so bad, does it?

Remember two important things about GPS data: Distance is measured in a straight line directly from you to the target; and with the turns, hills, and *switchbacks* of ground travel, the actual distance to the cache may often be significantly farther than the distance indicated on your GPS receiver. The compass bearing and pointer arrow also give you a straight shot to the target. Rarely can we ever follow an exact compass bearing unless flying or sailing, because there are fewer obstacles in the open sea and air.

GEO-LINGO

Switchbacks are areas on a trail that zig and zag up and down steep slopes. Although indirect, switchbacks help protect the incline from erosion; they also create a more gradual climb to the top of the hill. Always follow switchbacks when hiking.

We are off and running. The GPS is plugged into a power source to save batteries. Sure enough, after some time spent driving, the distance slowly starts to tick down. Only 15 miles to go, and when we turn on the main road, the pointer arrow is generally pointing in your direction of travel. Two roads will take us to the general area of the cache. After careful inspection, however, we find that a creek runs between the closest road and the cache site. From the map it's difficult to determine how big the creek is. That thin blue line could be anything from a dried up riverbed to a raging river. You decide to take the turnoff that requires hiking a little farther, but that's okay. It's not a race. It's all about the journey, the challenge, and enjoying the outdoors.

When we take the turnoff, the distance changes to 4.1 miles. We keep driving until we are about a mile away. If we continue up the road, the distance stops decreasing and starts to increase. So we turn around to park at a turnoff, estimating this is about as close as we are going to get from the road. Sure enough, there is a trail heading off in the general direction of where we need to be, which is also the direction toward the cache as indicated on the GPS receiver. It is now time to grab our gear, including a day pack with plenty of water, supplies, and spare batteries.

NAVIGATIONAL NUGGETS

A GPS receiver will not provide you with directions to a geocache, only distance and compass bearing. Remember there are 360 approaches to each location (one for each compass degree). The shortest distance may not be the most accessible or wisest path to travel.

Ground Search

We flip through the GPS receiver's pages to find a helpful one. The trail does not appear on the receiver's basemap. The compass page is selected to provide a large pointer arrow and the distance to the target. In this case, we are .85 miles away with a compass bearing of 290° west. Onward we go, down the dusty, twisted trail as the distance indicator slowly ticks down. For the person holding the receiver and watching its arrow, it is tempting to walk in a direct line, following the pointer arrow, tripping over rocks and brush, even though a neatly groomed path runs right alongside the course.

Geocaching point one: You probably do not need to bushwhack (travel off-trail). This might be necessary when you reach the cache's general location, but not three quarters of a mile away. It's time to start thinking like the person who hid the cache. Would he stumble over nature's obstacles for nearly a mile even though a trail leads to the same location? Besides not tripping and falling on your face, there are other good reasons not to bushwhack. Staying on trails makes less of an impact on the local environment. You may be leaving tracks and needlessly breaking tree limbs. Besides, it is not fun to get tangled in trees, thorns, and blackberry bushes. This across-land travel will get you scratched up and make it easier to get lost (as you wander in foliage that may obstruct your view). Even animals know this; that's why they use the trails, too.

This is especially true for off-road driving. Whether on a mountain bike or four-wheel-drive vehicle, traveling off the trail marks the ground and damages foliage. Off-trail travel often leads you to obstacles such as boulders or ravines, which make passage difficult. That is why someone else has already made a trail going to the desired location. Also, if you do need help, taking yourself off the beaten path only makes it more difficult for someone to find and assist you.

We are getting closer now, less than a half-mile, but now the trail has switched back and is heading the wrong way. Excitement turns to confusion as the group questions whether we are on the right path.

Geocaching point two: Even though a road or trail veers off in a different direction, it does not mean you are on the wrong path. Often wilderness roads switch back and curve all over to reach their destination. When you are in this situation, you have a choice of two actions to take. One is to check your map to determine where the trail or road ends up. If your path is not mapped, continue to follow it out. Keep a close eye on the distance indicator to see whether you are walking closer to or farther away from the target. If you continually get farther away, it may be time to backtrack and reassess your direction.

NAVIGATIONAL NUGGETS

Check satellite reception often. This will give you a good indication of how accurate the gear is at any given time. Be sure to check the battery gauge at the same time. It is typically located on the same page.

In our case, we decide to follow the trail out to see where it goes. Despite its curving, it does continue to lead us closer to the geocache. Now, with 320 feet to go, our anticipation builds as we wonder what we'll find. The arrow leads us into a forested area filled with logs and rock outcroppings—many good places to hide a cache. There is overhead tree coverage, and we wonder how good a signal we can get. We wander into a rocky, tree-covered area and continue until we get a reading of 41 feet. Going farther on the trail only increases the distance, so we turn around for another look.

No cache and no big "X" on the ground: This might be a little harder than we thought. Turning back around, we walk until there is a reading of 39 feet. This is still not as close as we would like to be, and the tree coverage is most likely affecting our GPS unit. This is a good time to check satellite reception.

We remember the receiver's satellite status page contains three indicators to check the potential accuracy. First, it indicates the number of satellites received. Under the trees, we have only four. Second, it indicates the EPE, estimated position error number. Our reading indicates that our receiver could be inaccurate up to 42 feet. The third indicator is the DOP, dilution of precision reading. Our number is 3.1. These numbers indicate that the tree coverage is definitely affecting accuracy.

After walking around the area, we narrow the location enough to start a ground search. Eureka! A plastic box is tucked away in a hollow log. In this case, we didn't use the encrypted code. Later, after decoding the message, we see that it reveals that we should look for a hollow log. We are glad we found the cache without the hint. That was a great search. We got to go for a hike and had fun looking around rocks and trees until we found the cache. We congratulate ourselves and take a group picture with the cache's disposable camera. The treasure we liberated was well deserved.

We found it!
(Jack W. Peters)

At the Geocache

Remember the rules: Take something, leave something, and enter your name and experience in the logbook. You worked hard to find it; it's your right to leave a record of the experience.

Now it's time to seal up the cache and place it back where you found it. If it was hidden in a stump or covered with rocks, place it back the way it was. Do not move the cache or leave it exposed. You want the next person to enjoy finding it also.

Sharing Your Experience

When you get home, log onto Geocaching.com and record your adventure for the world to see! A geocache log can be as detailed as you like. The cache owner is always happy to know about the condition of the cache and how well you enjoyed the experience. Also, if there were problems with the cache your log will tell the owner that cache maintenance is needed. This will allow future cache seekers to see when it was found and possibly learn from your experience. It may even help other geocachers decide whether this is the type of cache they want to visit.

There are five log types available when logging a cache:

- **Found It.** Used when the cache has been found and the log signed. Logging a cache in this manner increases your find count by one in your profile on Geocaching.com.

- **Didn't Find It (DNF).** Used when a search has been made but the cache could not be located. This type of log is useful for alerting cache owners of potential issues.

- **Write Note.** Notes are often used on return visits to a cache, perhaps to pick up a Travel Bug or simply check on it. At times, a note is used instead of a DNF if your geocaching adventure is interrupted and you don't want to give others the impression that the cache is missing.

- **Needs Maintenance.** Used if a cache is in need of attention from the owner. Maintenance can include replacement of a container, or even the need for a new logbook. Use of this log type places a Needs Maintenance attribute on the cache details page, which remains until the owner posts an Owner Maintenance log.

- **Needs Archived.** Used when the cache cannot or should not be replaced due to outside forces, including new construction, land-management issues, or other dangers. When a log of this type is posted, the local cache reviewer receives notification of it and may take action to archive the cache. Use this log type sparingly and only in situations where you are certain of the problem at the cache site.

Hiding a Geocache

So you have found a few geocaches by now, and it's time to move up the geocaching food chain. No longer just a seeker, you are now ready to join the elite ranks of those who hide geocaches. Great! Read on to learn how to place a geocache that you and fellow seekers will be proud of.

The first step is to research a cache location. Geocaching is just like real estate—location, location, location! It is common for geocachers to hide caches in locations that are important to them, reflecting a special interest or skill of the cache owner. When thinking about where to place a cache, keep these things in mind:

- **Does it meet Geocaching.com's listing requirements?** Make sure to review these during your research. Issues of concern include cache saturation, commerciality, solicitation, and long-term cache maintenance.

- **Did you consider accessibility?** If a cache is too visible or too close to busy roads and trails, there is a good chance someone may stumble upon it by accident. It is best to place a cache just off trail to preserve the environment but keep it out of sight of people casually passing by.

- **Did you seek permission from the landowner or manager?** If you place a cache on private land, you must ask permission before hiding your cache. If you place it on public lands, contact the land manager to find out about any rules or restrictions.

- **Will the location placement cause unnecessary concern?** Please use common sense when choosing a location for your cache. Do not design your cache such that it might be confused with something more dangerous.

As the owner of your geocache, you are ultimately responsible for it, so make sure you know the rules for the area where you place your cache.

Finally, try to place a geocache in a location that is unique in some way—a location, possibly challenging and scenic, that will leave a lasting impression on its visitors. Ideally, the site itself will be as great of a reward as finding the cache. Use your imagination and think of some of your favorite outdoor spots. A prime camping spot, great viewpoint, unusual location, etc. are all good places to hide a cache.

Container Considerations

You have many options for containers; the primary requirement is that they hold up to the elements. Depending on your climate, the container will have to hold up to rain, snow, dust, and heat. Often, containers are camouflaged to blend in with the natural environment. This makes them more difficult to find, especially by someone who might stumble across one by accident.

> **EUREKA!**
>
> Geocache containers can be nearly anything that is durable and watertight. They can be as large as a 5-gallon bucket or as small as a film container.

Geocachers have had good success with clear, watertight plastic containers, ammunition boxes, and waterproof boxes often used on boats. Micro caches are often plastic film containers or some other type of small waterproof capsules, usually just large enough to contain a small logsheet. Others are made out of fake rocks, mint tins with magnets, and waterproof match cases. To determine which type of container is most appropriate, consider where you will be placing it.

An example of clearly identified, watertight geocache containers.

You'll also want to invest in some plastic zippered baggies. These help you to organize the cache contents and help protect them if the container leaks. Whichever type of container you choose, be sure to identify your cache so that someone who doesn't play can figure out what it is. We suggest that you mark the outside of your geocache container with "Geocache" or "Geocaching.com," and the name of the cache so that it is easily identified as a geocache and not something dangerous. It's a great idea to include an information sheet explaining what a geocache is and contact information for if it needs to be moved. This data may help keep it from being ransacked or removed by someone who does not know what it is. Check out the Cache Notification Sheet in Appendix E. Make your own copy to laminate or place in a waterproof bag. Geocaching.com has a list of cache notification pages that have been translated into many different languages for placement in a variety of different countries.

Next you'll need a logbook and a pen or pencil. A small spiral notebook does the trick. If the cache is in an area that will freeze, use a pencil; pens can freeze and refuse to work in the cold. Be sure to place the logbook and pen or pencil in a plastic bag. Now it's time to stock the cache with goodies. Chapter 2 includes lots of ideas about what to include in your geocache.

When you place the container, never bury it. However, it is okay to cover it up with rocks, bark, moss, and dead branches. Concealing the cache a bit helps keep it from being found by *muggles.* Place the container in a hollow log or stump, or secure it with a heavy log or rock to decrease the chances of it blowing, floating, or washing away.

GEO-LINGO

Muggles are nongeocachers, usually people on the trail who look suspiciously at a geocacher on the hunt, or who have accidentally found a cache. Geocachers borrowed the term from the *Harry Potter* series, in which it refers to a nonmagical person. Muggles are often puzzled but are usually harmless. Geocachers often try to avoid being seen by muggles to keep the geocache safe from curious potential plunderers.

Saving the Coordinates

After the geocache has been placed, it is time to save the coordinates as a waypoint. If you haven't already, be sure to come up with a unique name for your cache. You'll use the name when saving the waypoint. Saving a waypoint is easy. Press and hold the Enter button on your GPS receiver until a new waypoint screen appears. Title the waypoint to match the name of your cache. You will have to abbreviate it because most receivers limit your title to only six digits or letters.

If your receiver has an averaging feature, use it to record the most accurate waypoint possible. This feature allows you to take the waypoint's reading over a span of time, usually a minute or two, to improve accuracy.

If your receiver does not have this option, you can use a couple of tricks to do it anyway. One is to save multiple waypoints of the same area; however, this is more effective if done over time. Selecting the waypoint in the center averages the position. You can use this same technique with the Track Log feature. Leave the receiver on to record a track log. After some time, zoom in to the recorded track log "blob" and save the center as a waypoint.

Just as when you entered a waypoint to find a cache, save your waypoint in the same format. Be sure to use decimal minutes and the WGS 84 map datum in North America. After you have your waypoint, it's a good idea to write it in permanent marker on the container and logbook, and make sure you have a copy to bring back with you.

As covered in Chapter 4, it is time to go online to post your new geocache for the world to find. When you post a cache, it is up to you to make sure all the information is correct. No one from a geo-caching website will personally go outdoors to review the site before approval. When a new cache is submitted, it is reviewed for inaccuracies, bad coordinates, and appropriateness before being posted on the web.

If you hide it, will they come? You will find out soon enough.

The Geocache Review Process

When a geocache is submitted on Geocaching.com it is placed in the Review Queue and marked for the volunteer reviewer of that particular area. Volunteer cache reviewers are geocachers who have been asked by Groundspeak to fulfill this role for the website. They are all geocachers themselves who love the game and have become familiar with the guidelines for placing a cache as well as special considerations in various areas as to land use and regulations.

Normally a cache reviewer examines your submission within one to three days (remember, though, that reviewers are volunteers with their own jobs and responsibilities that must come first). The reviewer examines the submission with a variety of maps and tools provided for the job and also keeps a keen eye on the guidelines that you read before submitting a cache. It's not uncommon for an experienced reviewer to catch a mistake or omission on your page and ask you to make changes before continuing the review.

Many of the concerns your reviewer might raise can be alleviated by giving attention to the surrounding area and the maps. If there is a trail system that used to be a railroad track but the maps still show it as a track, post a reviewer note with those details and any others that your reviewer might ask you about. This will greatly expedite the review process.

If there are any concerns, the reviewer will address them and wait for your response, otherwise they will push the magic Publish button and your geocache will be available for the world to see! Either way, you will be notified by e-mail when your geocache is published or if the reviewer needs more information from you.

Care and Feeding of Your Geocache

After you place the geocache, it is your responsibility to maintain the cache and the area around it. You need to return as often as necessary to ensure that your cache is in good shape and is not having a negative impact on the area. After it has been visited, it is a good idea to check with the geocachers who found it to ask their opinion of its condition and placement. Have a look when you can to make sure it is in good condition and stocked with trade items. If you have concerns about the location, discontinue the cache site and move it to a better location. When the geocache is active, it can remain in place as long as you or someone you appoint will manage it.

Ask Permission

Always ask permission before placing a geocache, especially on private property. Most sites have postings that indicate who owns or manages the area. Chances are they may never have heard of geocaching. It is up to you to explain the activity of geocaching, your role as a cache owner, and their potential positive contribution to the worldwide geocaching community. Obtaining permission from land managers is very important and helps ensure that geocachers will have a positive experience at the location.

Be aware that the U.S. National Park Service does not allow geocaching on the property it manages. In fact, it considers caches violations of federal regulation. These strict regulations are intended to protect the often fragile, historical, and cultural areas they manage.

> **DEAD BATTERIES**
>
> As the geocache owner, it is up to you to ensure that its placement and the foot traffic being brought into the area do not cause problems or environmental damage. If you realize the geocache is in a poor location, discontinue the site immediately and relocate it to a better location, or remove it entirely.

Do's and Don'ts

As mentioned before, the geocaching community is a self-regulating group. There are no geopolice to ticket you for placing a bad cache or leaving behind inappropriate trade items. Something even worse would happen: The game and its participants would start getting a bad reputation for being careless with safety, or possibly damaging the environment. This type of reputation would do nothing but cause geocachers to be viewed negatively, resulting in bad press and the closure of areas to geocaching. Geocachers know this, and, with minimal exception, have gone out of their way to ensure that geocaching goes on without causing concern or problems for others. Here are some important points to remember:

- Read the guidelines for placing a geocache before actually placing one. This will also save you from a lot of extra work.

- Use common sense when thinking about a location for your next geocache. Consider the possible impact it could have on the local area. Remember that your cache could attract a number of visitors.

- Clearly identify your geocache by marking the container with at least the cache name and GC code. This will help to avoid having the cache be mistaken as anything other than a geocache.

- Do not bury caches or leave them in areas that will cause damage to the environment.

- Do not place a geocache in any area that's home to rare or endangered species and plants. Also avoid areas with delicate ground cover: consider the number of people that may visit the site to find your geocache.

- Do not place geocaches on archaeological or historical sites. These areas could be negatively affected by the extra traffic the cache may cause.

- Do not leave behind any inappropriate material or items such as alcohol, tobacco, weapons, or drugs.

- Do not place a cache too close to an existing geocache. This can lead to confusion and oversaturation problems. Geocaching.com uses .1 mile (528 feet) as the standard minimum distance that must be maintained between geocaches.

- Do not leave a geocache in an area posted "No Trespassing."

- Do not place geocaches in areas that would be perceived to compromise public safety or cause unnecessary concern, such as near railroad tracks, public buildings, or military installations.

- Do not place a geocache while on vacation; you need to be available to maintain it on an ongoing basis.

- Do not place geocaches that solicit customers or are perceived to be posted for religious, political, or social agendas. Geocaching is supposed to be a light, fun activity and not a platform for an agenda.

The Least You Need to Know

- The decimal minute format is the most commonly used for geocache coordinates.
- Be sure to use the correct datum to avoid serious error.

- Know how to use maps and hints for assistance in finding geocaches.
- Geocachers should keep a geocache owner up to date on the status of her cache by logging their experiences online.
- Maintaining a geocache is the responsibility of the geocache owner.
- Always ask permission from the landowner or land managing agency before placing a geocache.

Geocaching Tips and Tricks

In This Chapter

- Advice for your geocaching adventures
- Learn techniques to find geocaches like a pro
- Learn how to keep yourself safe while on the trail
- What to do when encountering nongeocachers

At last you know how to geocache. You've learned how to use the web and how to get outside to seek and hide your own geocaches. Hopefully you've had the opportunity to experience the thrill of geocaching for yourself. If so, this activity could go beyond an occasional weekend pastime and become a full-blown obsession.

Have you been bitten by the bug to the point that you try to find ways to sneak out to get just one more cache? At night, are you looking around ferns and rocks in your sleep? We thought so. There is just one reasonable thing to do, and it's not therapy or counseling. No, it's time to go pro by learning from the best! We have assembled the best advice we could think of to help you find 'em fast and get you home by dinner.

Good Advice

Since geocaching is still a relatively new activity, many participants are self-taught and have learned what does and does not work through trial and error. The online geocaching discussion forums and face-to-face exchanges at geocaching events have also served to distribute some of the best geo-wisdom, tricks, and tips. By learning from others you can transform yourself from a stumbling newbie to a seasoned professional.

This chapter shares good, commonsense information about outdoor activities that will help you get out there and back in one piece. It also offers specific search techniques that will help make even the toughest geocache hides easier to spot. What do you tell nongeo-cachers you run into while on the trail? This chapter covers that topic, too.

Before You Leave

Tell someone where you are going. You can use the travel itinerary in Appendix F to leave vital information about the geocaches you are going after. Besides leaving the coordinates, let someone know whom you're traveling with, what communication gear you have, and what time you expect to return.

Bring a friend! It's always good to have someone with you when venturing outdoors. It's easy to have car trouble, get lost, or twist an ankle. Having someone with you can help overcome these challenges and get you back home safely. Besides, geocaching and the outdoors are always the most fun when shared with a friend.

Bring along a notepad and camera. You may see awe-inspiring areas that take your breath away. You will likely visit locations you have never seen before, and may not again if you don't take some notes. In the excitement of the moment, it's easy to forget the names of parks, trailheads, and waterfalls, or the unmarked turnoffs to get you there. Make notes and save lots of waypoints in your receiver. Don't forget extra batteries and film or data storage for digital cameras. A light-weight tripod works great to allow everyone to get in the frame if no one else is around to take a photo for you. Taking pictures is a great way to document your trip and enjoy your travels again and again. It's also fun to post your photos on the geocache's online detail page to share with others.

Outdoor travel often takes longer that you might think, especially if you are venturing out to unknown territory. When planning your trip, be realistic and give yourself enough time to get there and back.

Geocaching can be more fun when you bring a friend.
(Bernard Voges)

The problem with being caught outdoors longer than you plan for is that it gets dark. A day trip with a wrong detour can easily turn into a night trip. Always make sure to bring at least one flashlight with a spare bulb and batteries.

There is nothing worse than leaving for a trip only to realize you forgot something. Organize your navigation and outdoor gear in the same place. Appendix G is a helpful gear checklist.

Print out the geocache's information page and maps to take with you. This is important in order to check coordinates and hints if you get stumped. Don't forget to bring something of value to leave behind in the cache and a pen for writing in logbooks. Also, be sure to bring along plenty of water.

On the Trail

Do not spend too much time staring into your GPS's screen when you're driving to the trail. If you do, two things will happen: you will miss the beauty of the natural surroundings, and sooner or later you'll get into an accident. Have your passenger check out the screen while you're driving.

DEAD BATTERIES

Whether walking, riding, or driving, taking your eyes off the road to watch the receiver's screen too often could ultimately lead to an accident. Be careful or your friends will have to use the coordinates to call in the paramedics.

Before heading out on foot for a geocache, save your vehicle's location as a waypoint. It's easy to get disoriented, even when using GPS. Having the trailhead saved as a waypoint provides you a location to navigate back to.

Pay attention to where you're going and be aware of the surroundings. Occasionally, stop and make a 360-degree turn to study the landmarks around you and to get a reverse perspective of the landscape behind you. It's important to do this so that you know what the landscape will look like on your return trip. Besides major ground features, can you see the sun or moon? Recruit assistance from others to help keep track of where you're going as well as your location on a map.

Respect the land by treading lightly. Do not leave tracks or break foliage, and carry along a garbage bag to make it easy to pack trash out. Remember to practice Cache In Trash Out. The best way to travel through outback areas is by leaving no trace. You can find more information regarding principles of leaving no trace at www. lnt.org.

Map Considerations

Use the general map on the geocache details page and a roadmap to determine how to reach the cache area. When you're there, it's time to get serious with highly detailed topographic maps. Topographic maps are often referred to as 7.5-minute maps because the distance they cover is 7.5 minutes long and wide in latitude and longitude— approximately 55 square miles. These maps are typically very detailed in the 1:24,000 or 1:25,000 map scale. For example, in the 1:24,000 scale, 1 inch on the map equals approximately 2,000 feet on the ground. Book, outdoor, and travel stores are all great places to find topographic maps. They're a great investment for about $4. The digital topographic maps found on the cache details page are based on these maps.

After you learn how to read a map, you'll enjoy the challenge of following your position on it. Wilderness roads such as those marked by the U.S. Forest Service use small numbered signs. With a little practice, you can easily spot and match those signs in the field to the roads listed on your map. This proves especially helpful if you're traveling in areas where satellite signals are blocked by overhanging trees or cliff walls.

A map ruler enables you to plot your coordinates to a paper map, or take coordinates from a map to enter them as a waypoint into a GPS receiver. Also, consider using a map case to keep your new map dry. These are often clear vinyl sleeves that work great to protect a map and allow you to mark on the cover using a grease pencil or a dry-ink marker. Chapter 11 covers maps in detail.

NAVIGATIONAL NUGGETS

A map ruler is useful for plotting geocache coordinates on a highly detailed 7.5-minute topographic map.

Do Your Homework

If you get stumped trying to find an elusive cache, double-check the hint posted on the cache details page. A bit of overlooked data might just solve the puzzle. You can find clues in the general information about the cache, as well as the encrypted primary hint. There may be photos to check and spoiler information in geocacher logs that will give you that extra advantage in tracking down the tough geocaches.

It helps to know what type and possible color of container to look for. You already know you're looking for a container, but you gain a psychological advantage if you have a more specific idea of what type of container it is.

Search Techniques

More often than not, when you get close to the geocache, you're simply going to have to look around. Sometimes you can search for long periods of time and still not find a thing. Seasoned geocachers have been there. In the rain and in the heat, they have spent hours looking around rocks, trees, and foliage only to be stumped. Then when it all looked grim and they were ready to call it a day, their eyes caught something that didn't quite fit in the natural environment—a glimpse of plastic or metal that loomed out from the flora and fauna. You'll experience the same thing when your eye is trained on what to look for.

It often helps to think like the person who placed the geocache. When looking for a cache, ask yourself, "If I was hiding a cache here, where would I put it?" Geocache hiders can get very creative, but there are typically four main hiding areas in the outdoors: under a log, in a stump, under limbs, or under rocks.

Here are some helpful tips when closing in on a geocache:

- Check the satellite status page on your GPS receiver when you are within 300 feet. This will give you an idea of your accuracy for approach. Remember that the receiver may not direct you to the exact location. Depending on signal strength, 40 feet may be your closest reading.

- After you get close, your pointer function will no longer be accurate due to your slowing pace. The GPS receiver's compass feature does not function properly unless traveling more than 4 miles per hour. Because of this factor, when you slow down, disregard the pointer arrow and focus on the distance reading. You are now using what geocachers call *The Force.*

GEO-LINGO

After a little experience geocaching you will begin to notice your eyes being pulled almost instinctively to a little pile of sticks here or an oddly positioned rock there. Geocachers call this **The Force** and owe many finds to its mysterious power.

Cloverleaf

The cloverleaf is a search technique to use when you're close to the geocache and the pointer arrow feature is no longer accurate due to your slowed pace. The cloverleaf works by narrowing down the search area using the distance reading on your GPS receiver.

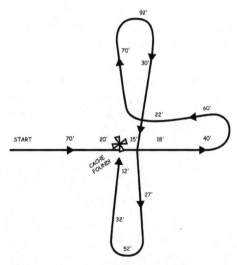

A cloverleaf pattern narrows the search area by moving in and out of the potential search location following the closest distance reading from a receiver.
(Groundspeak)

As you approach the geocache location, the receiver indicates a distance at the closest point, typically ranging from 40 feet down to 1 foot. If, as you move through the area, the distance increases, turn around and head back to the area where it decreases. Take off in a different direction until the distance increases, and then turn around and go back to the area that provides the smallest distance number.

Circling around in a cloverleaf pattern narrows the search area by further confirming the location of the closest reading from at least four different directions. Found the geocache? We hope so. When searching for a geocache, remember to always be aware of your physical location; your search method should not negatively impact the environment.

Triangulation

Triangulation is similar to the cloverleaf search pattern, except you use a compass to take bearings on the search area. When you slow down or stop, the pointer arrow on your receiver will no longer work properly but the bearing to the waypoint should still be accurate. This procedure works great for dramatically narrowing down the search area.

EUREKA!

Geocaches in urban settings present their own share of challenges. Because of the location, they are typically small micro caches that can be difficult to find under the watchful eyes of muggles. Be patient, take in your surroundings, and learn to pretend to tie your shoe. After searching for a few of these you'll get the knack for finding the most likely hiding spots.

As you approach the geocache location, check the bearing degrees and distance. Using your compass, take a bearing. Be sure that the magnetic reading of both the GPS receiver and compass match, either true or magnetic north. The receiver will most likely be set as a default to true north, although the receiver can provide bearings on true or magnetic north (an option you can set through the Setup menu). Use the true north setting on your receiver if your compass can be adjusted for declination to indicate true north. If your compass cannot be adjusted, or if you do not know how to make the adjustment, set the receiver to provide bearings in magnetic north. It makes no difference what format you use as long as both the receiver and compass are set the same.

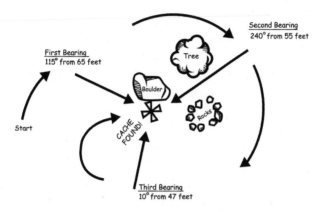

Triangulation narrows the search by taking three or more compass bearings on the target location.
(Groundspeak)

In our example, we approach the cache area and check the receiver data as we get close. We see the following:

> Distance 65 feet, Bearing 115°. Using a compass, we take a bearing in that direction. Looking carefully along the bearing, we see that it is just to the right of a large boulder.

> We circle the area clockwise to take a second bearing pointing west. The receiver indicates: Distance 55 feet, Bearing 240°. Along this bearing we see the path goes between a tree and rock pile, just to the left of the large boulder.

> The third bearing is from the south pointing north: Distance 47 feet, Bearing 10°. From this angle, the bearing is to the left of the tree and appears to be pointing at the large boulder.

> From these three bearings, all paths seem to point to the base of the large boulder. Sure enough, we find a plastic tube hidden in rocks exactly where the paths of the three bearings intersected.

In Life There Is No Reset Button

Thankfully, there are still beautiful outdoor places where Mother Nature and the order of the food chain still rule the day. Most of us have become far too civilized for our own good, and we can easily underestimate the power of nature. Safety should always be a major concern. Outdoor skills do not come naturally: they are acquired through education and experience.

It is your responsibility to have the knowledge and equipment to tackle the area you want to travel. This means being realistic about your limits to ensure you're not exceeding your outdoor abilities and putting yourself and others at risk. If you are leading a group, consider their limits, and remember they are relying on your knowledge to get them safely there and back. Make careful use of the terrain and difficulty ratings as well as the attributes on the cache page to eliminate any caches that might be beyond your or your group's comfort level. If you are unsure about more remote travel, take the time to educate yourself to build the skills and confidence necessary to make each excursion a successful one.

The rest of this section provides details about potential hazards and how to deal with them. Use common sense, think through challenges, and make the best decisions possible. This is done by not overestimating your abilities and by making cautious choices. Obviously, this book can't provide the exact solution to every potential problem, but here are some guidelines to help get you back from searching in good spirits and in one piece.

Environmental Concerns

The weather is typically the primary concern when geocaching. Being caught in a storm or in blazing heat unprepared and unprotected will definitely make you uncomfortable. Extended exposure can cause serious health problems and even death. Exposure is one of the leading causes of outdoor-related injury and death.

Hypothermia is caused by extensive heat loss, often a result of extended exposure to freezing temperatures, rain, and wind. The victim's body temperature lowers to dangerous levels, resulting in the body's inability to regain its own heat. It is estimated that hypothermia is responsible for 85 percent of outdoor-related deaths.

DEAD BATTERIES

Hypothermia kills because most people never realize they are experiencing it until it is too late. How can you tell if you're suffering from hypothermia while you still have time to treat it? Try touching your thumb to your little finger on the same hand. One of the first signs of hypothermia is trouble with dexterity. If you have difficulty passing this simple test it's time to get inside and get warm.

Heat exhaustion and, eventually, heat stroke are risks in warmer climates. The body temperature rises to dangerous levels from ongoing sun exposure and dehydration. In cases of cold and heat exposure, victims are subjected to extreme weather conditions for much longer than their provisions allow for. They often find themselves in such dire circumstances because they are lost or stranded.

Here are some ideas that will help prevent you from finding yourself in a worst-case scenario with the climate:

- Tell someone where you are going; give that person your travel itinerary.

- Wear the right clothing for the environment and climate.

- Bring the right gear for the environment and climate.

- Bring communication gear appropriate for the area.

- Bring and consume adequate amounts of food and water.

- Have some form of shelter available that is capable of protecting you from the elements.

- Take the proper steps to avoid getting lost.

Poison, Stingers, and Fangs

Out of all the potential outdoor dangers, being bitten or stung is probably the most common and annoying. Okay, getting attacked by a bear would be worse, but animal attacks are rare. It's the insects that are more likely to give you fits. Mosquito bites on sunburned skin, tripping over a hornet's nest, a spider in your boot ... you get the idea.

> **EUREKA!**
>
> "Gators" are protective wraps that cover the lower leg from the knee down to the top of your boot. They are ideal for hiking through brush or snow to keep thorns, insects, dirt, and other crud out of your socks and boots. Some are armor-plated to prevent snakebites.

Here's some advice to keep you from scratching your skin away:

- Learn what poison oak and ivy look like and stay away from them.

- Wear pants and long-sleeved clothing, and use insect repellent.

- Carry a first-aid kit that includes a snakebite kit.

- Always watch where you're walking.

- Check your sleeping bag, clothing, and boots before slipping into them.

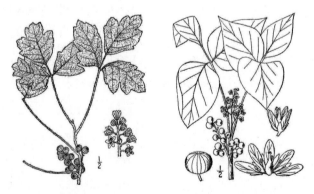

Learn what poison oak and ivy look like and stay away from them.
(Pbritt, N. L. & A. Brown, Kentucky Native Plant Society)

Dangerous People

Sometimes the most troublesome critters are of the two-legged variety. Although most people you meet in the outdoors are friendly and would go out of their way to help you, there are a small percentage of people whose intentions may not be good. Maybe they are opportunists who might steal your gear or mess with you if they felt they could get away with it. An even smaller percentage of people are downright outlaws. They use the woods to hide out or for illegal dumping or drug operations.

While geocaching, you might run across one or more people who appear to be a little shady. Long-term campers and land squatters often look rough, but might be perfectly harmless. If you are unsure about anyone you meet, the best thing is to just smile, wave, and leave. Don't be rude or tell them anything unnecessary like, for instance, that you're traveling alone. Regardless of what kind of jungle you find yourself in, criminals typically avoid people who do not appear to be easy targets or victims.

If you run across what looks like an illegal activity, immediately turn around and leave the way you came in. Remember the location and report it to the local authorities. Do not investigate the scene. Drug labs and dumpsites contain hazardous chemicals, and drug labs and marijuana crop locations are sometimes booby-trapped. Wilderness management agencies have their own law enforcement divisions for investigating such crimes. It is critical to report these crimes for a number of reasons. This activity is a serious threat to others and the environment. Such activity gives landowners and managers good cause to deny access to wilderness areas. Remember to keep the following in mind to stay safe:

- If you run across someone who you think may be unfriendly, just leave.

- Most criminals do not mess with people who look aware, confident, and capable of defending themselves.

- Immediately back out of any areas where criminal activities are taking place and report them to the police.

How Not to Look Weird

When you're geocaching, you are on a serious mission. You have a cold look of determination in your eye as you shake off the elements and obstacles that get in your way. Others who are on a nice quiet scenic getaway might not share your enthusiasm—not because what you're doing is wrong, but because they have no clue as to what you're doing. Curious onlookers may wonder why anyone would so intently look around the same area when nothing appears to be there. You will undoubtedly run across nongeocachers. They're everywhere. At some point, depending on their interest level, you may have some explaining to do.

Some geocachers are happy to share the activity with everyone they meet, enthusiastically explaining what they are doing and how to play the game. Many people find the idea as interesting as you first did, and who knows, maybe you just created a new geocacher. Others like to be a little more discreet. For them, part of the challenge is to get in and out without anyone else even knowing they were there.

Whatever you do, keep a low profile. People visit outdoor areas for peace and quiet, and there is no reason to disturb anyone else's tranquility. There is also no harm done in explaining what you're doing. Even if you do not want to take the time to do so, it's better than having others become suspicious of your behavior. Some geocachers have developed creative ways to mask their activity. They've used excuses ranging from being agricultural inspectors to doing some kind of research. Other geocachers have suddenly pretended that their GPS receiver is a cell phone and they are just having a phone conversation. Some even carry clipboards or wear hardhats knowing that such accessories can enable you to blend in and look like you belong there and are just doing your job.

Does this sneakiness help or just increase suspicion? Remember that what you're doing is a legitimate, family-friendly activity and that you do not want to cause anyone alarm. Here are some ideas when communicating with nongeocachers:

- Be prepared to quickly and politely explain what geocaching is. Most people receive the information with great interest.

- Remain low-key. There is no reason to disturb anyone or make anyone wonder what you're doing.

- Do not say or do anything that would make you appear as if you are doing anything suspicious or illegal. This is never more true than when you are approached by authorities.

- Be careful about how you use your receiver. In some countries, under certain circumstances, you could be considered a spy.

- Take out your trash bag and pick up whatever litter you find around the cache area as you search. Passers-by will generally ignore you, and if you're approached the conversation will most likely start on a positive note.

The Least You Need to Know

- Find geocaches like a pro by learning to think like a geocacher. Where would you place a cache in the same location?

- Take responsibility to learn outdoor skills and try not to exceed your abilities.

- Be polite and diplomatic with nongeocachers you meet on the trail.

- Remember, you can also seek the advice of seasoned geocachers by posting questions in the online discussion forums at Geocaching.com.

Geocache Types and Variations

In This Chapter

- Types of geocaches explained
- Playing other games with your GPS receiver
- Including geocaching games at outdoor events

If variety is the spice of life, it is the soul of geocaching. In this chapter you will learn how, in just a few short years, geocaching has evolved and even inspired the creation of a few new games that build on GPS technology and our love of exploration.

How boring would life be if vanilla was the only ice cream flavor? Likewise, geocaching has varieties that appeal to different people's interests. As you become more comfortable with geocaching, you may want to try all of the varieties.

The variety in geocache types and hiding places has grown due to the ingenuity of geocachers. The fun begins with that little-known, tucked away spot that only you know about. It continues with your own creativity in choosing a cache size and hiding method. Finally it is realized when other geocachers find your cache and share their experiences and suggestions.

Geocaching is fueled by imagination and is tempered only by the guidelines that govern geocache placement. By understanding the different types of geocaches, you can experience or create unique geocaching adventures for others to share.

At the Heart—Traditional Geocaches

The first geocache was a five-gallon bucket buried up to its lid in an orchard in Oregon. By today's guidelines, that cache would have never been published due to it being buried. As geocaching evolved, certain restrictions were put into place to alleviate the environmental impact and calm the fears of land managers who were worried about people digging for "buried treasure." This hasn't detracted from the fun of seeking out hidden treasures, though. If anything, it has given us a framework that sets geocachers' expectations when hiding and finding a geocache.

In its most basic form, a geocache consists of a container and a logbook. This is simply known as a *traditional cache* in the Geocaching. com pantheon of geocache types. The finder follows a set of coordinates that leads directly to the geocache, which was hidden using one of a variety of methods. While the process sounds straightforward enough, it's the individual creativity that each geocache owner puts into the cache placement that makes finding the cache a unique experience.

A smaller container, called a micro cache, is too small to contain items besides a log but is still considered a traditional cache.
(Georg Pfarl)

A traditional cache should be able to be found using the coordinates alone. This, of course, does not diminish the need for a good hint or other details on the cache page. Due to the clear-cut nature of this cache type, though, geocachers should know they're not going to have to solve any puzzles or do any compass work to get to the cache.

Multi-Caches

Multi-caches lead geocachers to two or more locations, the final location being a physical container. The intermediate locations can be either a physical item, such as a small (micro) container or a tag with coordinates to the next step, or a plaque or monument with numbers that lead to the final geocache. Multi-caches can also be *offsets*, which provide compass points and directions leading from a chosen location to the actual hidden geocache.

Multi-caches can be as simple or as complicated as you like. While most of them range from 2 to 5 steps, there are some that contain 20 or more and take some time to find. Putting a complicated multi-cache together can be a lot of fun but be aware that multi-caches of this kind may not be found as often. Also, make sure you will be able do the necessary maintenance on a cache with several steps.

As with all physical caches, multi-cache stages need to be kept at least 528 feet (that's .1 mile or 161 meters) away from any other geocache or stages of another multi-cache. This is to avoid getting caches confused and oversaturating the area with caches.

When seeking a multi-cache it's a good idea to keep notes on each stage. Make sure you read the clues carefully and change the coordinates when needed. It's very easy to miss one minor step in a multi-cache and find yourself searching in the wrong location.

Mystery or Puzzle Caches

As geocaching has grown, the challenge of the game has changed in many ways. Some geocachers love to go beyond the simple "follow the arrow to the hidden container" of the traditional cache and create mysteries and puzzles that not only offer finders a geocache as the payoff, but also offer the sense of accomplishment that comes with solving a puzzle.

You need only look at the number of people on the watchlist of a good mystery cache to realize what kind of attention these caches generate. They are often the topic of discussion at events and in local e-mail lists. As you search out mystery caches you'll come to appreciate the experience and creativity that a good puzzle creator puts into his or her cache. You'll also come to realize that many mystery and puzzle caches are simply variations on themes:

- **Number puzzles.** These are popular due to how easily they lend themselves to establishing a set of coordinates for geocaching. You'll find a lot of puzzle caches built around number games, such as Sudoku.

- **Word puzzles.** Like secret messages sent from spies, word puzzles can lead you to a set of coordinates using particular words or phrases as the keys to the puzzle. Some word puzzles might use a simple alphanumeric substitution (a=1, b=2, c=3, etc.) while others can have you searching for much more complicated patterns within the cache page.

- **Picture puzzles.** Do you know the order of the U.S. presidents? Are you familiar with semaphore flags? How are you with the periodic table of elements? All these are fodder for some great puzzles that have people at home doing lots of research before they hit the road to find a cache.

The mystery and puzzle cache types are also a great catchall for a variety of challenges and requirements that cache owners place on their geocaches. By seeing the familiar question mark icon of the mystery cache, a geocacher knows that he or she is going to need more than just coordinates to find the cache and will need to consult the cache information page.

When hiding a mystery or puzzle cache, keep in mind that the posted coordinates are rarely the actual coordinates for the cache. Instead they lead to the general area of where your cache is hidden (usually within two miles). From there the seeker must use the clues you've provided to locate the cache.

Letterbox Hybrids

Almost 150 years before the first geocache was hidden, people in Dartmoor, England, were hiding little boxes along walking trails and leaving clues for others to find them. The boxes often contained postcards and letters from visitors, so they became known as *letterboxes.*

Today letterboxing remains popular; there are geocachers who are also letterboxers and find that both activities provide a great amount of fun.

Letterbox hybrids are geocaches that contain many of the same properties as a letterbox. Like modern letterboxes, these geocaches contain a rubber stamp so seekers can record their visits in their own personal logbooks. The instructions on the cache page often resemble the series of instructions for finding a letterbox (for example, "From the last fencepost, walk 17 paces northwest, turn 90 degrees") but also contain coordinates that lead directly to the container. Sometimes letterbox hybrids are cross-listed on letterboxing websites. This provides a great way for geocachers and letterboxers to be introduced to each other's favorite pastime.

Letterbox   Webcam   Traditional   Project A.P.E.

Wherigo   Multi-Cache   EarthCache   Virtual

Some of the various geocaching icons that represent the different types of geocaches.
(Geocaching.com)

Virtual Caches

Virtual geocaches are intended to bring the seeker to a unique location, not to find a cache container. The location itself is the reward in this type of cache. These sites are typically of a unique landmark or historical monument. There are no containers, so nothing is traded except photos and experiences. Geocachers prove they were at the location by answering a question related to the area or by taking a photo of themselves.

Virtual geocaches are no longer published on Geocaching.com, but many have been grandfathered in and are still listed online there for you to find. Virtual caches were also the inspiration for another Groundspeak GPS game called "Waymarking," which will be discussed in Chapter 15.

EUREKA!

In 2001, 20th Century Fox placed 12 geocaches, called Project A.P.E., as a promotion for the movie *Planet of the Apes*. Each cache represented a fictional story in which scientists revealed an "Alternative Primate Evolution." These caches were made using specially marked ammo containers. Each cache had an original prop from the movie. Only a few Project A.P.E. caches exist today and many geocachers travel far and wide just to search for them.

Webcam Caches

Webcam caches use existing webcams that are available to be viewed by the public that were placed by individuals or agencies to monitor various areas like parks or roads. The idea is to get yourself in front of the camera to log your visit. The challenging part, however, is that you need to call a friend to look up the website that displays the camera shot. You must ask that friend to save the picture to log the cache. If you're a tech-head, you could use your wireless modem and save the image yourself on your laptop.

As with virtual caches, these are no longer published on Geocaching. com. But, like virtual caches, many webcams can be visited and logged on Waymarking.com.

EarthCaches

EarthCaches are a unique kind of virtual cache that gets you outdoors and learning about the world around you.

An EarthCache site is a special place that people can visit to learn about a unique geoscience feature or aspect of our Earth. Visitors to EarthCaches can see how our planet has been shaped by geological processes, how we manage the resources, and how scientists gather evidence to learn about the earth.

An EarthCache might take you to a cliff side where it would be necessary for you to count the different layers of strata in the rock you see. Or you might visit an artesian well and need to use a measuring device to record the flow rate. Visiting EarthCaches from various parts of the world exposes finders to the wide variety of geological formations on Earth. They're not only fun, but they're also educational!

EarthCaches are listed in conjunction with the Geological Society of America, but can be found all over the world—on land or at sea. Due to the distinct characteristics of EarthCaches, they are published under a different set of guidelines than other caches. Be sure to read up and follow all the instructions before attempting to place one.

For more information on EarthCaches, please visit www.earthcache. org.

Wherigo Caches

As the capabilities of handheld GPS units have evolved over the years, geocachers have been presented with new tools and opportunities. One of the most innovative new uses for GPS is an application called "Wherigo," which will be covered in depth in Chapter 16.

Wherigo is a toolset for creating and playing GPS-enabled adventures in the real world. By integrating a Wherigo experience, called a cartridge, with finding a geocache, geocaching can be an even richer experience. Wherigo allows geocachers to interact with a variety of physical and virtual elements that add to the adventure. These caches go beyond the capabilities of simple handheld GPS units and require more sophisticated units, which are discussed later in Chapter 9.

Benchmark Hunting

Benchmark hunting is searching for survey markers from a list maintained by the U.S. National Geodetic Survey (NGS). Benchmarks are geodetic control points that are permanently affixed objects at various locations throughout the United States. They are used for land surveying, civil engineering, and mapping. The NGS maintains a database of these locations, and each benchmark control point marker has a permanent identifier number (PID) and a datasheet of information about it. Many of these markers are old, and much of the descriptive data used to find them is outdated. There are, however, more than 700,000 of these markers within the United States, and they are still used today for the ongoing process of surveying our country.

There are two basic types of benchmark control points:

- **Vertical control points.** They establish the precise elevation at their placement point. They are typically small brass or aluminum discs, concrete posts, iron pins, or bolts permanently attached to a stable foundation.

- **Horizontal control points.** There are several names for these control points: triangulation stations, traverse stations, trilateration stations, GPS stations, and intersection stations. These, too, can be a small brass or aluminum disc, concrete post, iron pin, or bolt similar to the vertical control points. They can also be other features such as radio towers, water towers, church spires, mountaintops, or any other objects that can be identified from a distance.

> **EUREKA!**
>
> In the surveying profession, the term **benchmark** is applied only to the vertical control type; for benchmark hunting, however, we use the term for both vertical and horizontal control points.

Searching for Benchmarks

Searching for benchmarks to find is easy. On the Geocaching.com website, click on "Find a Benchmark" and search by postal code or point ID. A list of benchmarks will appear from the nearest to the farthest. A unique feature of benchmark hunting is that it does not require GPS. A receiver is helpful to get you in the right area, but then it's up to you to interpret the instructions on the benchmark's datasheet. Benchmark information pages from the Geocaching.com site do provide coordinates and directions.

A Bureau of Land Management marker found by a geocacher. Markers like this are used by land management agencies to mark locations and elevation.

(Bret Hammond)

Part of the challenge in searching for benchmarks is that the coordinates for the locations are usually not very accurate. Benchmarks were placed before the use of GPS, using coordinates plotted from a map, and may be more than a couple hundred feet away from the marker. Study the description and use the posted coordinates to determine the location.

If the benchmark page indicates that the location is "adjusted," you are looking for a horizontal control point that most likely has been plotted with highly accurate surveying-grade GPS equipment.

Finding a Benchmark

When you find a marker, do not tamper with it or take it. These markers are protected by law because they are public property and still actively used in surveying. Take pictures of the marker and the surrounding area, and then log your find at Geocaching.com. Don't forget to upload the photos to the website's gallery.

Some listings describe things like radio towers, church steeples, and smokestacks. These kinds of large-object station markers are known as *intersection stations*. They are usually landmarks taller than any surrounding objects, allowing them to be seen from many miles away in several directions. This makes them valuable points of reference for surveying.

When logging these benchmarks, keep in mind that in very unusual cases there is a benchmark disc, surveying nail, or other small object that can't be seen from the ground, the top of the tower, steeple, or smokestack. The datasheet will specify such a marker if this is the case. If not, simply log your find, and if you have a camera, take a picture of the structure from the ground. For safety and legal reasons, it is obviously best not to climb these structures.

Logging a Benchmark

When logging a benchmark, the choices are "Found it!", "Couldn't find it!", and "Post a Note." When you find a marker, be sure to double-check the description and datasheet to confirm it's the right one.

It's not unusual to find benchmarks that are not in the NGS database. This is because there are survey markers everywhere and the NGS is not the only organization that creates and uses benchmarks. Other agencies include the U.S. Army Corps of Engineers (USACE), the Bureau of Land Management (BLM), and other federal agencies, along with highway departments, county and private surveyors, and engineers.

DEAD BATTERIES

Use caution when seeking benchmarks. Some are located on private property or in hazardous areas. Also, remember these markers are very important for surveyors, engineers, and others, so do not tamper with them or take them.

You may log an official report to the NGS if any of these three points are met:

- When the description of how to get to the station marker has significantly changed.

- When a station marker has not been visited in a long time: 30 years or longer. You can find this information on each benchmark page in the description area. See a sample at www.geocaching.com/mark/details.aspx?PID=CG1067.

- When the station marker is obviously destroyed. "Destroyed," to the NGS, means that you found the marker and that it is obviously out of its installed position. If you cannot find the marker for any reason, don't report it to the NGS as destroyed.

NAVIGATIONAL NUGGETS

The NGS website (www.ngs.noaa.gov/) is an excellent resource for learning how to read datasheets. Review samples by clicking "Datasheets."

Make sure that the marker's history has not changed in the official database of the NGS before planning your report. Also, do not report benchmark coordinates to the NGS for any reason. The existing coordinates on the NGS datasheets cannot be changed, except through very rigorous mathematical procedures. Geocaching.com has additional instructions and information related to finding, logging, and submitting reports to the NGS. Learn more at www.geocaching. com/mark.

Degree Confluence Project

The goal of the Degree Confluence Project is for participants to visit each of the latitude and longitude degree intersections around the world. There is a confluence every 49 miles, or 79 kilometers. Even after eliminating confluences in the oceans and some near the poles, as of this writing, there are still over 10,000 left to be found.

Participants who visit intersections post photos of the intersections along with stories to the Degree Confluence website. If more than one intersection has been visited, every participant's personal story and related photographs are listed online.

For more information, visit www.confluence.org.

Adding Geocaching Games to Your Events

The possibilities for adding geocaching-style games to outdoor events are as endless as there are geocaches to find. Families, clubs, companies, and all kinds of organizations can liven up their picnics and events. This is being done now by a wide variety of organizations, ranging from Boy Scout troops to search-and-rescue teams to church groups. Outdoor skills trainers are also recognizing the benefit of these games as a practical and fun way to teach GPS and navigation.

Adding geocaching-style games to your next event is a great idea for a number of reasons:

- It's fun. Remember that? In our busy lives, especially in a corporate or organizational setting, how often do we get the opportunity to enjoy ourselves? It gives everyone something to do other than sit around and eat. It will intrigue your guests, leaving them with a positive experience they will be talking about later.

- It exposes people to GPS, navigation, and outdoor skills who otherwise may not have sought it out on their own. This includes those who have always wanted to learn about GPS but may have felt intimated by the technology. Geocaching provides an introduction to these skills, allowing them to determine whether they want to pursue the activity further.

Adding geocaching games to your events might be easier than you think. There are a couple of ways to do this. Do a search for geocaches in the area of your event and bring the information along with you. Most parks, picnic areas, and camp locations have caches hidden in and around them. The other option is to hide a few of your own. Geocaches could be filled with prizes or gift certificates that would have special meaning to the group. Be creative: A day-off pass would be popular at a company picnic, for instance.

Corporate team-building company PlayTime Inc. uses geocaching for its GeoTeaming program. After a brief classroom-style training session covering GPS, geocaching, and navigation basics, the group breaks up into teams that head out to compete for points by finding geocaches of various difficulties and distances in a certain amount of time. These programs are fun and educational, and help groups learn how to work better together to accomplish goals.

The Least You Need to Know

- Geocaching continues to evolve as an activity; there are many different types of geocaches that appeal to a wide variety of people.
- Benchmark hunting is a unique GPS activity that allows participants to seek survey markers that were placed and are managed by the U.S. National Geodetic Survey (NGS).
- Benchmarks should never be taken or tampered with.
- Geocaching-style games can liven up your next picnic or outdoor event.

Travel Bugs, Geo-coins, and Other Trackable Items

In This Chapter

- An explanation of Travel Bugs and other trackable items
- What to do when you find one
- How to place one of your own

Most geocachers are fascinated by travel and love to explore new locations. Yet, even in geocaching, there can be limitations to how much we can see and how far we can go. That's where Travel Bugs and other trackable items come into play. When we can't go to a location ourselves, it's fun to send something that represents us out into the world. In this chapter, you will learn how trackable items travel from geocache to geocache, picking up stories and photos along the way.

Message in a Bottle, Revised

In the early days of geocaching, a unique phenomenon was observed. Players were leaving objects in geocaches not for trading but for traveling. Instructions were placed with these trinkets to keep them moving from geocache to geocache. Finders of the trinkets would send e-mails back to the owners letting them know which geocache the item was now in and how far it had traveled. These trackable items came to be known early on as "hitchhikers."

Like a bottle drifting in the ocean, trackable items are objects that find their way around by drifting from geocache to geocache. These items are usually some form of toy, symbol, or trinket that has meaning to the person placing the item. Trackable items often include instructions for transport, either random or to a specific destination.

It's up to the owner of the trackable item to give it a travel goal or mission. A geocacher who finds a trackable item might be asked to relocate it to another geocache, take it somewhere special, or help it complete a journey or mission. Trackables can have goals to visit cities or countries, possibly traveling around the world. Each journey is unique, and trackable items can take on lives of their own.

Unlike a traditional message in a bottle that is never seen by the owner again, the unique feature of trackable items is that their adventures are tracked online. When a geocacher finds and relocates an item in the real world, she must also log the find online, sharing stories and/or photos relating to its relocation and travel. Each time an item is logged, the owner of the item is notified via e-mail and learns of its adventures. A written log and map of all documented travels for each trackable item is maintained online for all to share and enjoy.

Travel Bugs

With the popularity of hitchhikers, the staff at Geocaching.com came up with the idea of having geocachers attach dog tags with unique serial numbers to the items that move around. Serial numbers provided a much more efficient way to track their travels, and so the *Travel Bug* was born.

A Travel Bug dog tag is a metal tag with a unique tracking number available for lookup at Geocaching.com. It is usually attached to a hitchhiker, but can be used by itself. These bugs can be easily identified and viewed on the Geocaching.com site using their numbers. A geocacher who finds a Travel Bug logs information on how he found it and the new location so that the person who hid the Travel Bug in the first place can check on its current whereabouts. Every time a Travel Bug, or other trackable item, is logged, the owner of that trackable item receives an e-mail notice from Geocaching.com.

GEO-LINGO

Travel Bug is a term that was coined by Jeremy Irish of Groundspeak in July 2001, inspired by a person's "travel bug," or desire to travel. The term "Travel Bug" and the Travel Bug logo are registered trademarks of Groundspeak Inc.

A Geocaching.com Travel Bug dog tag.
(Groundspeak)

Each Travel Bug is stamped with the Travel Bug bar code trademark logo and an individual tracking number. Each Travel Bug includes a duplicate tag and a chain. Owners can keep the duplicate as a memento and a quick way to check up on their bug's status. The copy makes a neat necklace for hard-core geocachers, a great key chain, or possibly the ultimate accessory for your pet's collar.

Travel Bugs are usually attached to an object the owner thought would be neat to travel. Besides the object, which is often reflective of the owner's personality, each Travel Bug takes on an identity of its own. Each is named, has travel goals, and gets its own dedicated web page at Geocaching.com. Here is an example of a Travel Bug:

Name: 50 State Cruiser

Released: Friday, December 22, 2006

Origin: Kansas, United States

Recently spotted: In the hands of sabrefan7

Current goal: My mission is to cruise from state to state, visiting *all* 50 states grabbing up pictures from cool state landmarks or oddities.

About this item: This TB is a toy replica red and silver Honda 1000R street bike. Help it cruise along.

Finding Travel Bugs

If you find a Travel Bug, it is important to check to see whether the owner attached any instructions. Log on to Geocaching.com and go to the specific page for the geocache where the bug was found. Log your find, and then click the Travel Bug name link on the Inventory section on the page. Note that Travel Bugs are named. In the previous example, its name is 50 State Cruiser.

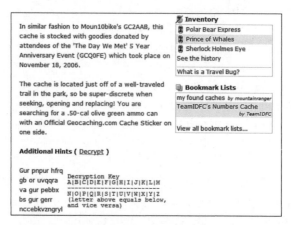

A Travel Bug link is shown in the geocache Inventory.
(Geocaching.com)

Clicking the Travel Bug link brings up the bug's dedicated details page. On this page, you can read all about the Travel Bug, including the description, owner's name, and travel goals.

If you can't remember where you found the Travel Bug, you can also look it up by the specific Travel Bug tracking code at www.geocaching.com/track/. This page also works for looking up any trackable item.

There are a few options available for logging a trackable item. If the item has been properly logged into a geocache, you can simply retrieve it from the geocache where it was found. However, occasionally Travel Bugs are misplaced or a previous geocacher will have forgotten to log it into the geocache. When this happens, you have the option of writing a "Grabbed it from somewhere else" log. This enables you to inform the owner that the bug is no longer missing in action but has been found and will continue its mission soon.

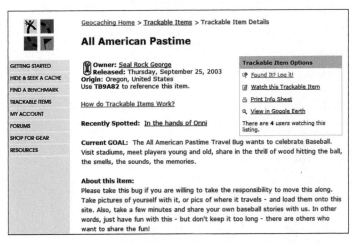

This page shows a Travel Bug's information, such as its name, owner, and travel goal.

(Geocaching.com)

Another logging option is to write a "Discovered it" log on the trackable item's page. A "Discovered it" log means you are not moving the item to a new location, but you can confirm that you have seen it in a specific geocache. This can be a very useful tool for the Travel Bug owner who might be concerned that the bug is missing if it has not been logged as having been moved from a geocache in some time.

"Discovered it" logs are also useful for Travel Bugs and other trackable items you might encounter at geocaching events. It's a nice way of saying "I saw you!" and lets the owner know that you appreciate her sharing her trackable item with you.

If you log a "Retrieved it" note, the trackable item will be shown in the online inventory on your personal account page. The next time you log that a geocache has been found, there will be an option to select the trackable item from your inventory list and post it to the new geocache location.

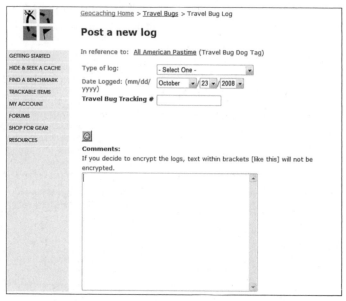

This page enables you to log a found Travel Bug after entering its tracking number.

(Geocaching.com)

Relocating Travel Bugs

When you move a Travel Bug to a new geocache, visit Geocaching.com and go to the new geocache's page. When you log the geocache as found, you'll see a drop-down menu at the bottom of the page that provides an option to select the Travel Bug from your inventory list and "attach" it to the new geocache. When you submit your log entry, the bug will appear on the new geocache's page and others will know that it is in the geocache ready to be found again. Don't forget to upload an image since most trackable-item owners love to see photos of their items traveling "in the wild."

> **EUREKA!**
>
> The first Travel Bug, Deadly Duck-Envy, was placed on August 31, 2001. As of this writing, there are many hundreds of thousands of trackable items in play.

Creating Your Own Travel Bug

Sending a Travel Bug on its way is a lot of fun! The first thing you need to do is purchase a Travel Bug from Groundspeak. These can be purchased online at www.shopgroundspeak.com. Once received, it is time to activate the bug. Log on to Geocaching.com and click the Trackable Items link on the left side of the screen. Enter the bug's tracking number under the Travel Bug icon.

The activation code is included in the Travel Bug package. Successfully entering the tracking number and activation code brings up the Travel Bug's information page. Enter the Travel Bug's name, starting city, activation date, description, and goal, and your trackable item will be activated and ready to go. Congratulations, it's all yours! Use the Edit link in the upper-right corner of the page to edit your Travel Bug's name, description, and travel goals.

Whether you are relocating a bug or activating a new one, you have an opportunity to upload images to a Travel Bug page. Click the Upload Image link. If you are the bug's owner and have loaded multiple images, open the bug's Edit page and a drop-down box will appear with a list of the images loaded. Select your favorite picture and it will become the image for your bug's dedicated page and entry in the Travel Bug photo gallery.

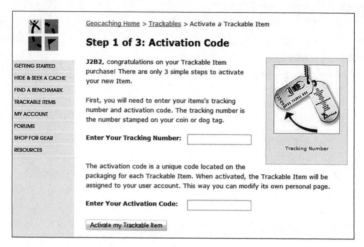

New Travel Bugs are brought to life by entering the tracking number and the activation code.

(Geocaching.com)

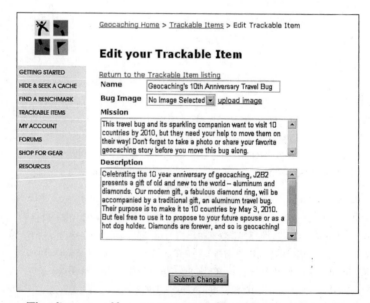

The edit page enables you to name your Travel Bug as well as to list a description and travel goals.

(Geocaching.com)

The Evolution of the Travel Bug

As with geocaching itself, trackable items and Travel Bugs have evolved much through the creativity of geocachers. What began as a way to identify trinkets that move from container to container has grown into a means of self-expression.

There are a whole horde of oversized Travel Bugs in the world that won't fit into most geocaches. Rather, these "travel beasts" make their way from geocaching event to geocaching event, where they are displayed and discovered by geocachers. Some of these Travel Bugs are so well-known it's considered an honor and somewhat of a status symbol to log them.

- **Cindy (the Cinder Block).** A standard 38-pound cinder block with instructions to be left near a geocache since it likely won't fit in the geocache. After five years and over 12,000 miles Cindy is covered in hundreds of signatures of the geocachers who have discovered or moved her.

- **Mary Proppins.** Mary is a propeller blade from a commercial aircraft. The owner gave her the goal of being moved by at least one geocacher. In nearly 9,000 miles of travel she's far exceeded his goal.

- **Chain Chomp.** A 15-pound bowling ball with a large chain attached. Considering the size and unwieldiness of a Travel Bug like this, it's amazing to realize it has traveled over 8,000 miles.

It's also not uncommon to attend events and see geocachers wearing T-shirts (or sporting tattoos) with their own personal Travel Bug tracking numbers. You will even find geocachers with pets and vehicles as their own personal Travel Bugs. Rather than move these from geocache to geocache, they are available to simply discover as a way of saying that you've met or seen them.

Coffee Bug was a Travel Bug released in Alaska in 2002. CYBret put it on his watch list simply because he loves coffee and hoped that their paths might cross some day. Imagine his surprise in 2007 when he finally crossed paths with it and was able to have a cup of coffee with the Travel Bug.
(Bret Hammond)

Geocoins: Trackable Meets Collectable

In the early days of the Geocaching.com website, a Washington State geocacher by the name of "Moun10bike" developed a new trackable that would eventually spread like wildfire. Jon Stanley (aka Moun10bike) donated many of the original software licenses used to run the Geocaching.com website. As a token of Groundspeak's appreciation, Jon was provided with the ability to have his "geocoins" tracked on Geocaching.com, just like Travel Bugs.

In no time at all, geocaches bearing Moun10bike trackable geocoins were immediately sought after. The coins themselves were traded into other geocaches and passed around the community. Being able to log one and get that coveted icon on your geocaching profile was a rite of passage among geocachers.

Soon people weren't only moving them from geocache to geocache, they were asking Jon for permission to keep the coins as collector's items. It quickly became apparent that something very special was catching on.

A short time later, mass-produced geocoins with their own icons became available as an alternative to Travel Bugs. But it was in 2005 that people started producing personal geocoins. Soon, geocachers were collecting and trading coins that reflected the distinct personalities of the geocachers who created them.

A collection of geocoins created by individual geocachers, groups, and organizations.
(Groundspeak)

Today, geocoins number in the thousands with more and more being created each year. Most of them continue to have their own individual tracking numbers and custom icons. Collectors love them not only for their value, but also for their uniqueness and quality. If you would like to create your own geocoins, you can learn more information at www.geocaching/track/geocoin. There, you will find answers to frequently asked questions as well as a list of geocoin manufacturers and resellers. If you attend a geocaching event you will often see the die-hard geocoin collectors off in a corner showing off their collections and making trades for that next "must have" trackable geocoin.

Travel Bug Stories

Travel Bug and trackable-item owners enjoy seeing their creations travel from place to place, each developing a story of its own. Unfortunately, some bugs get exterminated by being taken and never placed again, whereas others travel across many countries, for many thousands of miles.

Some of these bugs begin to stand out thanks to lofty goals or distances traveled. Following are examples of Travel Bugs that have found their way around.

Darth Vader TB1

Darth Vader TB1 is a typical-looking bug, a tag attached to a Star Wars toy. Its mission is also typical enough: "Darth is on a mission to find other Jedi out in the geocaching universe. Please help him get to as many states as possible by the end of the year. Alaska would be a really cool place to visit, as Darth's master has always wanted to go there, but he will take a trip to any exotic location anywhere in the geocaching world."

After Captain Prozac retrieved the bug, he took it along to the Gulf to fly seven combat missions over Afghanistan. After its share of combat service, it enjoyed a stop in the United Kingdom before returning to the United States. Of course, the bug accompanied the captain at a couple of pub stops along the way. The cool weather was a nice relief from the 100+ degree heat of Afghanistan.

After a whirlwind journey of an amazing 17,534.64 miles, Darth was returned to his owner and is now spending the rest of his days in retirement on the shelf.

Darth Vader TB1 on a combat mission over Afghanistan with a Navy fighter escort.
(The captain)

> **EUREKA!**
>
> Did you know that Travel Bugs are often used as teaching tools? From science and mathematics to history and geography, students can learn a great number of lessons, even predicting the Travel Bug's movements in the world!

Sysop's Traveler

When one of the founding members of the Little Egypt Geocaching Society (L.E.G.S.) in southern Illinois was killed in a motorcycle accident, the members knew they had to do something to honor the memory of their friend. Sysop loved wolves, so arrangements were made with a wildlife rescue organization to adopt a wolf. As a way of saying "thank you," the organization gave L.E.G.S. a certificate and a little stuffed wolf.

If there's one thing Sysop loved as much as wolves it was traveling, so they struck upon the perfect idea for the little toy wolf. They attached a Travel Bug tag to it and sent it out on a mission to visit the kinds of places Sysop loved to go. The geocachers who have picked up this

Travel Bug really seem to want to honor Sysop's memory. The stories and pictures they have placed on the bug page truly do reflect the spirit of their friend.

DEAD BATTERIES

Use good geosportsmanship when it comes to Travel Bugs and other trackable items. It is considered bad etiquette to remove an item from a geocache and not move it along to another geocache. E-mail the owner if you keep an item longer than a couple of weeks. Also, do not mail items to a destination. If you do, what's the point? The point of trackable items is to give them the most interesting journey possible.

Tigger

On September 14, 2001, only days after the September 11th tragedy, geocacher bigkid sent a Travel Bug on a special mission to the site of the World Trade Center. Its goal, "The wonderful thing about Tiggers is their power to heal and make fun. My name is Tigger Travel Bug and I'd like to go to New York City and help the people around the WTC by making them smile. Can you please take my picture at the location of the WTC? Then perhaps I can make my way back to Seattle."

On February 16, 2002, after thousands of miles of travel through the goodwill of geocachers, Tigger stood at the memorial viewing platform at Ground Zero in the hands of geocacher Perfect Tommy.

Tigger's Travel Bug page contains many touching photos and logs from his journey. Tigger finally returned home to Seattle 16 months after he left. He was attached to a Ground Zero 9-11-01 NYC knit cap. Tigger had traveled 7,022 miles and touched the hearts of many.

The Least You Need to Know

- Travel Bugs and trackable items are special trade items that are designed to move from geocache to geocache, picking up stories and photos along the way.
- The serial numbers on Travel Bugs allow them to be tracked on geocache and user profile pages at the Geocaching.com website.
- Releasing a Travel Bug of your own is as easy as registering its owner's name, the bug's name, and its traveling goals or purpose.
- Do not take a Travel Bug or trackable item if you cannot place it in another geocache soon.

Get in Gear

In the last few years we've witnessed a revolution in the development and use of GPS receivers. Once deemed a high-tech toy for only the most avid of users, GPS devices are becoming an essential tool in navigation and outdoor recreation.

However, if you're a more casual user, chances are you haven't completely explored the features of your GPS receiver. In Part 3, we discuss important functions and features of devices to give you a better understanding of what the technology can do.

We also give you the rundown on the GPS receiver options available so that you can buy the right gear for your needs and use. Then, it's time to set up your gear by finding out what all of those buttons are for.

As useful as GPS technology is, it doesn't replace the traditional map and compass. After you get your grid lines and true north figured out, it's time for some serious high-tech fun by exploring the use of GPS mapping and computers.

Choosing a GPS for Geocaching

In This Chapter

- Learn about GPS receiver features and options before you buy
- Choose the right type of receiver for your use
- Learn to select the right antenna
- Find out everything you ever wanted to know about batteries
- Check out our recommended features for geocaching

Ask 100 geocachers what equipment is needed to locate a geocache and you'll likely be provided with 100 different answers. That's because the equipment you use may vary depending on the frequency with which you go geocaching, the typical terrain, the weather or season of the year, and the number of geocaches you usually seek in a single outing. Therefore, the equipment you choose is going to be a personal decision based on your needs and affordability. This chapter covers the basic options available and provides GPS receiver recommendations by type and cost.

GPS Receivers

GPS receivers are manufactured in various shapes and sizes, with as many features and prices. GPS technology is used for so many different recreational uses that it can be confusing to know which unit to buy and how much money to spend to get the features you need. Remember to keep your intended personal use in mind so that buying the right gear will be a worthy investment.

EUREKA!

Secure your gear with a lanyard. They are great for attaching GPS receivers, cameras, and radios. If you drop your gear, you will likely save it from crashing to the ground. They're also great for keeping gear from becoming lost or stolen.

Fortunately, modern GPS receivers share many of the same features, regardless of price. Nearly any GPS receiver will work for geocaching, but some work better than others. Understanding the available features will enable you to make an informed purchasing decision. We understand that when you purchase a GPS unit, you will probably use it for more than just geocaching. Here is a list of the common features available. Learn how they may be applied to geocaching and other applications.

Primary Features

- **Accuracy.** Fortunately, accuracy is consistent in most receivers regardless of the style or cost.

- **Address finder.** Allows an exact address to be located within a basemap database.

- **Alarms.** An alarm notifies the user of an approaching waypoint. Text alarms flash a message on the screen; audible alarms sound a tone.

- **Altimeter.** A 3-D, four-satellite fix provides elevation information, although satellite-based altimeters are not known for being very accurate. Some GPS receivers provide a built-in barometric altimeter for more accurate elevation readings independent of a satellite connection.

- **Antenna jack.** This feature allows for a remote antenna to be attached. This works well for obtaining satellite reception if your GPS unit is mounted within a vehicle with no clear view of the sky. You can also bring it along while geocaching to get better signals under heavy tree cover.

- **Auto routing.** Provides turn-by-turn directions to a waypoint. Directions may be in the form of arrows, automated voice commands, or both.

- **Basemap.** Most recent-model GPS devices include a map database stored within their memory. Basemaps include general information on cities, roadways, and waterways. Basemaps typically include such large geographic areas as North America and the United Kingdom.

- **Battery duration.** Battery life is important for extended hikes with no other power source available. Receivers are rated for battery life duration for both continuous use and power-saver modes.

DEAD BATTERIES

Using a receiver without a basemap can be difficult when geocaching. If you do not have a basemap, bring along a paper map and try to plot the location coordinates. It is always wise to get a good sense of your final destination and best means to access the location before setting out to find a geocache.

- **Computer interface.** Data in/out capability allows the unit to receive (upload) data from a computer or send (download) data to a computer. This information includes digital maps, track logs, waypoints, and routes. NMEA, the National Marine Electronics Association, ensures that data can be exchanged with other electronic devices. If you plan to do more than a few cache hunts, make sure your receiver has this interface capability.

- **Durability.** It's not a question of whether or not you'll drop your GPS receiver, but of how often you'll drop it and what you'll drop it on. It's important that you choose a durable handheld model instead of something designed more for navigation inside a vehicle. Most handheld models come with rubber grips that will help you hold the device and cushion it slightly in a fall.

- **Electronic compass.** Although receivers provide compass data, the feature will not work in a stationary position. This feature is available to provide compass data independent of satellite reception. However, this feature drains batteries faster than standard GPS use.

- **Memory.** For receivers with a basemap, memory is used to store additional mapping data. GPS manufacturers provide greater detailed maps in CD-ROM and SD card formats exclusively for their brands. Map details, especially topography contour lines, use a great deal of memory. Some models have expandable memory, allowing virtually unlimited storage with high-capacity cards (or by storing multiple maps on more than one card). On some units, additional memory will enable you to store additional waypoints.

- **Routes.** A series of waypoints listed in sequence from start to finish. Routes typically contain up to 30 waypoints, although they may contain more. Designed to guide to a destination, they can also be inverted or reversed to track back from the destination to the starting point.

- **Sun/moon position.** Provides sun and moon positions, including sunrise and sunset time of day.

- **Tide page.** Provides times for high and low tides. Some caches are hidden on islands that can be accessed only by foot at low tide.

- **Track log.** Plots an electronic breadcrumb trail as a sequence of dots or trackpoints, showing a path traveled. Various brands and models provide different numbers of trackpoints that can be used. A backtrack feature automatically establishes a route from the last track log to provide a series of waypoints to follow on the way out.

- **WAAS ready.** These receivers are capable of accepting radio signals from the Wide Area Augmentation System (WAAS). These signals can increase the accuracy of your GPS unit to within 3 meters. However, this feature drains batteries faster than standard GPS use.

- **Water resistance.** Receivers are rated for their resistance to water. *Water-resistant* usually means the equipment can be splashed or briefly dunked (a rating of IPX4). *Waterproof* means the equipment can be submerged for a specific amount of time, such as 30 minutes, before damage occurs (a rating of IPX7). Regardless of rating, use a watertight box or bag if you use your receiver around water. Saltwater can kill electronics instantly.

- **Waypoints.** Specifically recorded locations stored within a receiver's memory. Saved waypoints enable you to return to exact locations. Various GPS brands and models enable you to store different numbers of waypoints. Most modern receivers enable you to store at least 500 waypoints.

- **Waypoint averaging.** A standard feature on most new GPS receivers. Waypoint averaging provides greater accuracy of saved waypoints because you actually record the position over a period of time. This is ideal when placing geocaches.

Device Types and Application

GPS receivers come in a variety of sizes and prices and provide various features. Devices can be generally grouped into the following categories:

Handheld Without a Basemap Database

These models are examples of low-cost, entry-level receivers. All work well and are capable of the same accuracy and provide the same features as more expensive models. These basic receivers are about the size of a TV remote control, with an approximate 2-inch view screen. They include built-in antennas and most likely do not include a remote antenna jack.

Garmin eTrex H.
(Image used courtesy of Garmin Ltd. or its affiliates. Copyright © Garmin Ltd. or its affiliates.)

Garmin Geko 201.
(Image used courtesy of Garmin Ltd. or its affiliates. Copyright © Garmin Ltd. or its affiliates.)

- **Price.** $99 to $180.

- **Pro.** Low cost, small and lightweight, many features, and simple to operate.

- **Con.** No basemap, points of interest only, which makes the receiver more difficult to use and requires the ability to read and plot map coordinates. These models often do not include a data cable or data port for transferring information from your computer.

- **Application.** Ideal for geocaching, hiking, and biking where size and weight are important. Purchase this type of receiver if low cost is a primary consideration.

Handheld with a Basemap Database

The next step up, these receivers include an electronic basemap.

They may include other features such as memory or the capability to accept a memory card to store additional mapping data.

Magellan Triton 500.
(Image used courtesy of Magellan Navigation, Inc. or its affiliates. Copyright © Magellan Navigation, Inc. or its affiliates.)

Garmin GPSMAP 76S.
(Image used courtesy of Garmin Ltd. or its affiliates. Copyright © Garmin Ltd. or its affiliates.)

- **Price.** $160 to $249.

- **Pro.** Electronic basemap provides a useful reference. Additional features may include external jacks for a remote antenna and a computer data cable. Memory storage capacity allows the use of the manufacturer's maps on CD-ROM or memory card. Some models may also include an electronic compass and altimeter capable of functioning independently of satellite reception.

- **Con.** Screen size works well for general handheld use, but the screens are difficult to read in a moving vehicle. While the basemap contains most major roads, many of the secondary roads you will be geocaching on won't be shown on your maps.

- **Application.** Ideal for all-around recreational use. Works well in vehicles through the use of a remote antenna.

Full-Featured Handhelds

The next generation of handheld GPS contains all the features you will need for geocaching and any other outdoor adventure you might find yourself on. Expandable memory for extra maps and waypoints is just the beginning. These machines can load geocaching data directly onboard, making them the one tool you need for totally paperless geocaching.

Don't let their features fool you, these are rugged waterproof devices made to tackle the great outdoors.

Garmin Oregon 400t.
(Image used courtesy of Garmin Ltd. or its affiliates. Copyright © Garmin Ltd. or its affiliates.)

Magellan Triton 2000.
(Image used courtesy of Magellan Navigation, Inc. or its affiliates. Copyright © Magellan Navigation, Inc. or its affiliates.)

DeLorme PN-40
Image used courtesy of DeLorme Inc. or its affiliates. Copyright © DeLorme, Inc. or its affiliates.

- **Price.** $399 to $699.

- **Pro.** Built-in worldwide color basemaps and topographic maps on higher end models. SD card slots for more memory. Barometric altimeters for accurate elevation readings. On top of this, some models feature built-in cameras and voice recorders, and many are capable of wirelessly transferring waypoints between units. Some models also feature touch screens, which means fewer buttons and larger screens. Integrated geocaching functionality.

- **Con.** For some people, price is a big factor in whether or not this is the GPS for them. Also, for the beginner, the wide variety of features can be confusing.

- **Application.** This is a geocacher's dream. As the game continues to grow and new features are made available, these devices will set the standard for the future of the game and the development of other GPS gaming, such as Wherigo.

Vehicle-Based Receivers

Various models of vehicle-based receivers are available. Their larger screens are also ideal for RV or marine use. They are typically mounted with a swivel bracket and hard-wired, eliminating the need for batteries. These receivers are more expensive, averaging $500 to $1,000.

This type of unit works great for traveling around, but is not much good for geocaching if you can't take it with you on foot. You can take some of these models with you, such as the Garmin Nüvi. The large color screen is great but it can be a bit delicate for field use. You might decide that a larger sized receiver is fine if you primarily use it mounted in a vehicle, but you can still take it with you when you go out on the trail.

Computers and PDAs

If you're already packing around a portable computer, there are options to convert it to a GPS receiver. Digital assistants, PDAs, or laptop computers can be used this way through the combination of software and an antenna. Handheld PDAs use an adapter sleeve with an antenna that plugs into an expansion slot. Laptops use a dash-mounted remote antenna. Another option is to use them wirelessly in conjunction with a Bluetooth GPS receiver.

Real-time tracking is another neat way to combine the use of receivers and computers. Various brands of mapping software will accept a GPS receiver's signal to display a user's location indicated as an icon centered on a PDA or laptop screen. Chapter 11 covers computers and real-time tracking.

- **Price.** $370 to $490 (software and antenna).

- **Pro.** Great way to utilize computer equipment and save money by using electronics already owned. PCs accept high-quality mapping software. Larger screen size with a greater memory capability at a lower cost.

- **Con.** Often a poor choice for geocaching because they are not as durable or weather resistant as regular GPS receivers. Laptops are limited to vehicle-based use due to size and power requirements. Unless you rig up a stand, a passenger is needed to hold the computer; in addition, the power and data cords can be cumbersome.

- **Application.** Computers are an excellent complement to traditional GPS gear. They are great for trip planning and managing waypoints and routes. Ideal for vehicle-based use. Perfect for executives and road travelers who already use mobile computer equipment.

Cell Phones

Over the past few years, we have witnessed significant developments in cell phone technology. Today, there are a multitude of cell phones out there with integrated GPS. With the addition of navigation software that uses the phone's built-in GPS, many cell phones can now be used for geocaching.

iPhone 3G running Groundspeak's Geocaching Application.
(Groundspeak)

- **Price.** $100 to $500 for the hardware, although cell phone carriers often subsidize the cost of a cell phone if you agree to a contract term. Geocaching applications can range from free to $25 depending on the feature set.

- **Pro.** Easy geocaching access without having to purchase a dedicated GPS unit. With data plans and associated coverage, you can have real-time access to geocaching information for spontaneous geocaching. If you already have the phone, spending $10 for a geocaching application is an inexpensive way to get involved. One less device to carry with you.

- **Con.** Cell phones are generally not as durable or weather resistant as regular GPS receivers. Navigation with GPS consumes battery at a high rate and makes full-day adventures difficult without recharging the phone battery.

- **Application.** They are great for spontaneous geocaching, which makes them perfect for anyone who is interested in on-the-go geocaching without significant planning.

Antennas

Would you watch a big-screen TV with poor reception? Imagine sitting through the big game or your favorite movie with a fuzzy picture and bad sound. You'll want good reception on your GPS receivers, too. No matter how good the equipment is, it will not function well without strong satellite reception.

As mentioned before, tree coverage, buildings, and cliff walls can stop reception dead in its tracks. Using a receiver on the dashboard of your vehicle usually doesn't work that great, either. Mounting a receiver or PDA on the dash or using a suction cup to attach it to a windshield will obstruct your view. Some windshield safety glass is lined with metallic substances that block radio signals.

Here's a list of the different types of antennas and how they are best used:

Patch or microstrip. Most handheld receivers include this form of built-in antenna; it is the most compact and durable type of antenna. This type is better at locking on to satellites overhead than to satellites on the horizon. For best accuracy, hold the receiver vertically.

- **Pro.** Durable, compact, and lightweight.

- **Con.** Reception might not be quite as good as the other options. A receiver with this antenna might not have a remote antenna jack.

Quadrifilar helix. This is a tube-style, detachable antenna that Garmin uses. It provides greater accuracy and can lock on to more satellites on the horizon. Best accuracy is achieved by adjusting the antenna straight up. Because the antenna is detachable, a jack is provided to plug in a remote antenna; you can also make the existing antenna a remote one with the use of a coax patch cable.

- **Pro.** Improved reception for increased accuracy. It ensures an antenna jack for going remote.

- **Con.** Can be more easily lost or broken.

External. Necessary for applications where equipment is mounted inside a vehicle. Most are powered, or "active." The amplified signal increases the ability to lock on to more satellites and compensates for signal loss due to an increased coax cable length. Use an antenna that is active. Passive, nonamplified antennas do not perform as well and can conflict with an internal antenna. Remote antennas can also be used on top of helmets or shoulder straps, allowing the GPS to be stored safely in packs. This helps protect the gear from being lost or damaged and frees up your hands. Under ideal conditions, a quality active antenna can pick up 11 or 12 satellites.

- **Pro.** Ideal for vehicle use. Active antennas provide the greatest potential to lock on to the most satellites possible.

- **Con.** They need to be securely mounted to prevent damage. They also need to be backed up with a standard antenna in case of failure.

Batteries

Batteries are the lifeblood of geocaching. Not only do you need extras, but when it's time to purchase them, there are more options than you might think. Choosing the right type will help squeeze a little extra mileage out of them and possibly save a little money, too. Here are the basics:

- **Alkaline.** These are typically the most common and eco-nomical to use. A quality set of these batteries lasts 12 or more hours in a receiver. They are also sold in bulk to reduce the cost further. Power is considerably reduced in freezing temperatures.

EUREKA!

It helps to use cameras, flashlights, radios, and other gear that use the same batteries as your GPS device. Active geocachers should also con-sider using rechargeable batteries.

- **Alkaline rechargeable.** They only last approximately 60 percent of the life of a regular alkaline, but they can be recharged effectively up to 25 times. Most rechargeable batteries have memory. Batteries last longer if they are com-pletely drained before charging.

- **Lithium.** These batteries are more expensive, but may last more than 30 hours in a receiver. A set of four costs approxi-mately $10. This style is ideal for low-temperature use.

- **Nickel-cadmium (NiCad).** These batteries may only have a life span approximately 33 percent of alkaline, but they can be recharged around 500 times. Economical to use, but plan on changing them every 7 hours.

- **Nickel metal-hydride (NiMH).** Similar to NiCads, but with an increased life span of approximately 75 percent of alkaline. The greatest benefit is that they do not need to be drained before recharging. NiMH batteries can be recharged from 500 to 1000 times under optimal conditions.

EUREKA!

Batteries can be lightly greased to prevent corrosion. This is ideal for longer term storage applications, such as in flashlights, or any use where the gear is exposed to moisture. Dielectric silicone is a commonly used grease for these purposes.

To save batteries, turn the receiver off when you are not using it. Using the screen's backlight burns power faster. Backlights are typically on a timer that can be programmed to stay on a reduced amount of time. Check the equipment's battery-level gauge frequently to avoid having gear go dead.

Special Considerations for Geocaching

Fortunately for geocaching, expensive and elaborate gear is not required. More importantly, gear should be easy to use, accessible, and durable. Outdoor gear gets seriously abused. Gear can get smashed in bags and packs, rained on, frozen, dropped in an icy river, and so forth. You get the idea. Luckily, most receivers are built to military specs to withstand a lot of electronic killing factors like moisture, dust, and vibration.

Here's a list of device feature considerations for geocaching:

- **Basemap.** This is highly recommended. The additional cost is marginal, and the increase in the equipment's usefulness is substantial.

- **Channels.** Most GPS units today have 12 parallel channels. Channels help to acquire GPS satellite signals faster and more accurately. If you are looking at older GPS devices, consider models built after 1997. Older, single-channel receivers are much slower and may not be as accurate.

- **External antenna jack.** With new GPS devices this has become less important because the newer chips are sensitive enough to acquire signal inside a vehicle. However, it is not always possible to obtain good satellite coverage through a front windshield; this is when an external antenna can help. Even backpackers will benefit from the ability to safely store the receiver inside a pack with an antenna attached to backpack shoulder straps. It can also help outdoor use in places, where signals are weak, such as those under heavy tree cover.

- **Interface.** If you are using the receiver with a computer, be sure that the receiver includes an interface cable so you can quickly load maps and waypoints onto your device. Newer GPS units often support USB while older devices generally have serial attachments. If you purchase an older GPS device and have a newer computer, you may need to purchase a USB to serial port adapter as well.

- **Memory.** This is used to load detailed topographic maps, street-level maps, or additional waypoints into the receiver. Detailed maps can use a great deal of memory on your device. Consider internal storage capacity. Higher end devices also usually accept a memory card for additional storage.

- **Power source.** It is preferable to have a device that can support external power, like a cigarette lighter power cable. Due to the power requirements the device should support standard batteries (AA or AAA) for easy replacement on the trail. Lithium batteries are recommended for newer GPS models to ensure a longer battery life, and power geocachers should consider rechargeable batteries.

- **Screen size.** For visual ease of operation, use a receiver with the largest screen that can be realistically carried. Screen size is measured diagonally. Color is great and helps define map features, and a backlight is important, although both features burn additional battery power. A screen protector is important in preventing scratches out on the trail.

- **Waterproof.** Sooner or later your gear will get submerged. Get gear that is at least water-resistant, although an IPX7 designation is preferred. Plastic bags and boxes give electronics a little additional protection.

It is also important to note that an increasing number of higher end GPS devices now have functionality specifically created for geocaching. These devices can store detailed cache information, including cache details, hints, and recent logs. Some also store field notes to help you log your geocaches while outdoors!

The Least You Need to Know

- Consider how you will be using your gear and take the time to learn about all the various features and options available.
- Geocachers should shop for GPS receivers that are durable, waterproof, and compact.
- GPS receivers with built-in maps, external antenna jacks, and power cords are typically worth the extra cost.
- Making an informed buying decision will save time, money, and possible aggravation.

GPS Setup and Features

In This Chapter

- Explore GPS device buttons and screens
- Learn how to set up a new receiver properly
- Use the simulator mode to program settings without wasting battery power
- Navigate with ease by learning how to use waypoints, track logs, and routes

Now that you own a GPS receiver, it's time to actually learn how to use it! The information in this chapter in no way replaces the owner's manual, but provides additional explanation so that you can quickly and confidently head outdoors.

In this chapter, we will learn to use basic device features to program your gear to play. After the basics are out of the way, we will then get down to the specifics of using GPS by saving waypoints, track logs, and routes.

Learning Your Way Around Your Receiver

As much as we love high-tech gear, it can be intimidating. Most electronics have more features and buttons than you will ever use. That's fine, but you still need to learn the basics. Learning new functions and features opens up new possibilities, and familiarizing yourself with the device will quickly increase your confidence in navigation.

DEAD BATTERIES

This information is not intended to replace your equipment's owner's manual. Take the time to study the operation of your device to comfortably know how to use it. Read this chapter side by side with your receiver's manual before you head out, and take the manual along in a waterproof bag.

Fortunately, the major brands of GPS receivers share most of the same features and commands, although they may work a little differently. Studying this information with your product's instruction manual will provide a better understanding of how your device works.

Spend some time getting to know the purpose of each button and screen and practice using its features before relying on your device in the field.

Which Button Does What?

You can expect to find several kinds of buttons on most GPS receivers. Here's a list:

- **Enter.** This button is used to select options from menus and to save waypoints.

- **GoTo or Nav.** This button allows the selection of a waypoint from a list of waypoints saved within the receiver's memory. Holding this button down in an emergency saves a "man overboard" (MOB) waypoint on most, if not all, units.

NAVIGATIONAL NUGGETS

When using steering/guidance screens or pointer arrows, it is nearly impossible to maintain the exact bearing unless traveling by air or water. Roads and trails usually require you to track in different directions before reaching the destination. They are helpful, however, to determine if you're on track, and are the major indicator used in geocaching.

- **Page.** This button scrolls through the receiver's set of data screens.

- **Power.** This button turns the equipment on and off and may be used to adjust the screen's backlight.

- **Rocker keypad.** This button is used to move around on the map page and to select options from menus.

- **Zoom.** This button is used to change the viewing scale on the map page. "In" provides a more detailed smaller-scale view. "Out" provides a larger-scale view.

Common Pages

There are several types of pages you can expect to encounter on your GPS receiver. Here are some common ones:

- **Active Route page.** Once a route is selected, it displays the list of waypoints in the route and indicates which waypoint is currently activated.

- **Compass page.** Used for steering guidance, this page provides a compass ring and pointer arrow. If a waypoint is selected, the arrow will point to its bearing. An arrow pointing straight up indicates you are on course to reach the waypoint. The compass ring typically indicates the track, the direction actually being traveled. The compass reading will not be accurate unless the receiver is moving at least four miles per hour. In a stationary position, a bearing number should be accurate, although a regular compass is needed to determine the bearing's direction.

  The compass page, with its large pointer arrow, is the primary screen used to find a geocache.

- **Highway page.** Also used for steering guidance. A picture of a moving highway runs down the page indicating an upcoming waypoint, or group of waypoints if using a route. To stay on course, keep the highway down the center of the screen.

This screen is most helpful when straight-line navigation is possible.

The Compass page provides direct bearing to a geocache or anywhere else you might like to go.
(Images used courtesy of Garmin Ltd. or its affiliates. Copyright © Garmin Ltd. or its affiliates.)

- **Information or Position page.** Multiple data fields providing whatever information is programmed to appear. A wide variety of data can be programmed to appear in a series of fields. Take the time to review the various information available to determine what data is the most useful to your application. The following are some typical data fields:

    - Altitude

    - Average speed

    - Bearing

    - Course

    - Current coordinates

- Distance to next

- ETA to next

- Pointer arrow

- Speed

- Sunrise/sunset

- Time of day

- Time to next

- Track

- Trip odometer

- Trip timer

- User timer

- **Map page.** Primary display page that indicates your location with a present position pointer icon pointing to your direction of travel. The screen shows your movement in real-time with a history in the form of a track log. The screen may be orientated to be displayed with the top of the page indicating north or the direction of travel.

- **Satellite Status page.** Provides the number and signal strength of the satellites received. Includes Estimated Position Error (EPE) and Dilution of Precision (DOP) number readings to estimate accuracy. Provides current navigation status such as: Searching, Acquiring, Poor Coverage, 2-D Navigation, or 3-D Navigation. It also typically includes a battery-level gauge.

The best way to familiarize yourself with your device is to simply turn it on and check out the features. Go outside and get a satellite fix, then scroll through and explore the pages. One of the most commonly used pages is the Map page. Your current location will be displayed in the center of the page by a present position arrow icon.

If your receiver has a rocker keypad, use it to move the cursor arrow around the map screen. A data field box will display changing coordinates and the distance from your current location. This is useful for finding approximate distances to nearby locations. Scroll to a nearby city and check out the bearing and distance. The distances provided are direct as the crow flies. Unless traveling in a straight line, mileage needs to be increased to estimate actual distance on the ground.

If your receiver includes an electronic basemap, you can view it in greater or less detail by using a Zoom feature. When initially viewing the Map page, the present position arrow icon will be in the center of the screen. The bottom of the screen will include a distance indicator that shows the scale of the current map. Zooming in will increase the map's detail. Roads and waterways and their names will appear as you zoom into an area of the map. The zoom range may go from 2,000 miles to less than 500 feet.

Setup

Before using the gear in the field, take time to carefully review the owner's manual to make some choices. The following sections summarize what to consider when selecting setup options.

Alarms

Alarms can be set for a specific time or waypoint arrival, and to notify if you are off-course. When the alarm activates, a text message will appear on the screen.

Backlight Timer

The backlighting on the map screen uses a good deal of power. If operating on batteries, set the light to remain on just long enough to view the screen. When using a direct power source, it is helpful to keep the light on.

Battery Type

Enter the type of battery used to ensure the greatest level of accuracy from the battery-level gauge. Installing batteries also resets the battery-use timer.

Coordinates

The coordinates setting determines how coordinates will be displayed. There are various options available based on your location and preference. The two primary geographic coordinate systems are latitude/longitude and Universal Transverse Mercator (UTM).

Latitude/longitude is displayed in degrees, minutes, and seconds. The selection may look like HDDD° MM' SS.S". The standard for geocaching is the minutes displayed with a decimal point without the use of seconds. This display looks like HDDD° MM.MMM".

UTM is metric and displays in meters. Its selection looks like [UPS/ UTM]. The UPS is the UTM's system to grid the North and South Poles.

Distance Measurement

Distance and speed can be measured in statute or nautical miles. The receiver may also display metric kilometers. Note that a nautical mile is equal to 1.15 of a regular statute mile. A kilometer is equal to .62 of a statute mile, and a statute mile is equal to 1.6 kilometers. Based on your selection, altitude will display in either feet or meters.

Map Datum

The receiver will have been set as a default to one of the common map datums, such as the one used for geocaching, WGS 84. In North America, other common datums include NAD27 CONUS and NAD83. Remember to set the receiver's datum to match topographic maps. Note that there are a number of options for NAD27. The primary datum used in North America is CONUS.

Map-Page Orientation

Map-page orientation sets the direction of the map page. North Up orients the top of the page to north despite the direction of travel. Track Up changes the top of the page to the direction of travel.

North

The type of north can be selected for your preference. The following are the options available:

- **Auto Mag Var.** Magnetic north automatically adjusts for local declination (the same reading as a compass).

- **True.** True north.

- **User Mag Var.** Adjustable to any degree of declination.

NAVIGATIONAL NUGGETS

Remember, if working within a group, be sure everyone is speak-ing the same navigational language. Agree in advance on the following, and then set your GPS receiver to the correct values:

1. Map coordinates—lat/long or UTM? If lat/long, full address or decimal point?
2. Which north—true or magnetic?
3. Which map datum?

Time

Time of day is adjusted to display regular 12-hour time or 24-hour military time. The time provided is exact and set to your local time when you enter your time zone, or how many hours before or after UTC time (also known as Greenwich Mean Time or "Zulu time") your location happens to be.

Timers

A trip computer can be used to track average speed or minimum speed, or provide an odometer for your overall travels or for a particular trip. Timer features also include a user timer and a battery-use timer. Remember to reset these fields before setting off on a new trip.

NAVIGATIONAL NUGGETS

Most GPS receivers provide a Trip Computer feature. Reset the computer before your next outing to check out interesting data. This includes trip odometer, average speed, trip timer, and maximum speed.

Save Your Batteries with Simulation, Demo, or GPS Off Mode

These modes save valuable battery power by allowing you to review and program information without the receiver searching for satellites. This proves helpful when learning how to use the device indoors; you can learn without the device trying to obtain a constant satellite fix. Without the receiver searching for satellites, the battery power requirement is reduced by nearly half.

In this mode, you can review, demonstrate, and program the receiver's various functions and features. It is ideal for transferring data with a computer and for updating and entering waypoints and routes. Despite not using a satellite fix, navigation calculations can still be made. For example, waypoints can be entered as a route to determine the bearing and distance between waypoints.

Unfortunately, the Satellite Status page may appear as if satellites are being received. This is only an example of what the Satellite Status page looks like under normal operating conditions. The device's location will most likely appear as the last area for which the receiver obtained a real satellite fix. Be sure you are not in simulation mode during normal navigation operation.

Saving Waypoints

One of the primary reasons to use a GPS receiver is to save and travel to waypoints. This, of course, is the whole basis of geocaching; the geocache's coordinates are saved as a waypoint.

Besides telling us the distance and compass bearing, the receiver's computer can provide neat information we have never had access to before. An estimated time of arrival (ETA) is provided based upon our current speed.

The first waypoint to save is your home. This is helpful, because regardless of where you are in the world, the waypoint can be recalled to determine how far in distance you are from home and the time to return there. Venture out to the yard for a satellite fix.

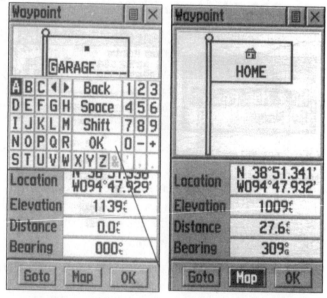

The best waypoint to save first is your own home location.
These Garmin screens show the waypoint name and symbol being selected.
(Images used courtesy of Garmin Ltd. or its affiliates.
Copyright © Garmin Ltd. or its affiliates.)

The present position pointer icon appears in the center of the Map page. Holding down the Enter/Mark button will give the option to save the current location as a waypoint. A mark waypoint screen appears and provides a new number such as 001. Using the rocker keypad or up/down buttons, select the letters to change the default number to the name "Home." On many GPS units, you must press the Enter button between each letter or number saved. Most receivers provide at least six characters, letters, or numbers for saving waypoint names. This screen also displays the date the waypoint was created and the coordinates of the location. A symbol can also be selected, which is helpful to label and organize waypoints. In the preceding example, the house symbol that will appear on the Map page screen is selected.

The waypoint screen shows a list of locations saved.
(Image used courtesy of Garmin Ltd. or its affiliates.
Copyright © Garmin Ltd. or its affiliates.)

Saving waypoints is important because it gives you a perspective of your travel area. Save lots of waypoints; your receiver will probably allow you to store 200 to 500 or more, and you can always delete old ones. Save your campsite, the trailhead, where you park your truck, and your favorite picnic area or swimming hole. If you ever do get turned around, select the nearest waypoint you need to navigate to. You can select the waypoint page and select a waypoint, or press the GoTo or Nav button, and the screen will ask you what waypoint you want to go to, possibly the nearest or most recently saved. It's that simple; getting lost has never been so much fun. Even in a worst-case scenario with your batteries going dead, you can use your compass and hike out on the bearing provided with the selected waypoint.

Saving waypoints is a fun way to document your travels. Better yet, you can share them with others. There are a number of ways to save waypoints:

- **Entered manually.** Geocaching style number one, the numeral coordinates are entered manually using the rocker keypad or up/down buttons.

- **Marking the current position.** This is one of the most common and easiest methods. Holding down the Enter/Mark button, as in the home example, saves the current position.

- **Selecting from a basemap.** Using the rocker keypad, the cursor arrow is moved to a desired location and then saved with the Enter/Mark button. Note that holding down the button too long may result in saving the current location instead of the planned position. Double-check the coordinates to ensure you did not save the current location. Using this same method with a Garmin unit and pressing the GoTo button will result in a waypoint titled "Map." This option puts the receiver into a GoTo navigation function to this location.

- **From a computer.** Geocaching style number two, previously saved waypoints and routes are loaded from a computer to the receiver. This is done through selecting a computer interface data-transfer option within the receiver and the use of a data cable.

- **Name search.** Most receivers provide the option for a name search of towns and cities. When the location is selected, pressing the GoTo or Nav button creates the location as a waypoint.

- **Mark a MOB position.** On many receivers, holding down the GoTo button saves a "man overboard" waypoint. This is a quick one-button method ideal for emergency situations, as indicated by the method's name.

- **Enter a projected position.** Compass bearing and distance information is entered in the reference fields on a new waypoint screen. This data can be entered from a current position or any other waypoint. From these values, the receiver projects the new location and saves it as a waypoint. Some of the more difficult geocaches require this function.

NAVIGATIONAL NUGGETS

Holding down the GoTo or MOB button on most receivers saves the current location as a "man overboard" (MOB) waypoint. This feature is designed as a one-button method for immediately marking and navigating back to a location.

After waypoints have been saved, the data can be modified at any time. The name, symbol, and coordinates can be manually changed or deleted.

Waypoint Averaging

As mentioned before, it is helpful when hiding a geocache to improve the accuracy of the coordinates you provide for it by averaging a waypoint. After saving a waypoint, press the Menu button. If your receiver includes this function, a menu will appear asking whether you want to average this waypoint. Press Yes and a numbered counter will appear. This indicates how many seconds of averaging has taken place. Obviously, the longer you average, the greater the accuracy. You may want to set the receiver down during the averaging process. Then come back in a few minutes and press Enter. The screen will provide an estimate of accuracy within feet or meters.

Track Logs

A track log is an electronic "breadcrumb" trail that is stored and displayed by the receiver. This log indicates the path you have traveled, greatly reducing the chance of becoming lost. Following a previously stored electronic track allows you to literally retrace your steps to backtrack to a previous position. This feature requires two elements to work properly. First, there must be a continual satellite fix for the duration of the track. If coverage is broken, blanks will appear on the track, which will most likely be represented as straight lines. The second element is that adequate memory be available to record the track.

Many receivers are somewhat limited in storage capacity. Depending on the unit's setting, one of two things will happen if the track log memory becomes full. The receiver will stop recording or it will automatically delete older track data. Most receivers provide the option of programming the track log as follows:

- **Fill.** This option records track log data until the memory is full. A text warning message may appear when the memory is full. This option is useful when returning to a starting position is most important.

- **Wrap.** Under this option, data is continually recorded. This is done by recording over the earliest saved data. This option is useful when the latest saved data is most important.

- **Off.** This may be useful to prevent recording excessive tracks to be saved on a log. Shutting this feature off presents a risk because no tracks will be recorded if you fail to turn it back on.

NAVIGATIONAL NUGGETS

Track log data is valuable to geocachers because it does such a good job of documenting your travels. Zooming in on the Map page will show tracks in greater detail, which may help you to find a geocache by indicating that you have walked a specific area.

Another variable is how often a track will be recorded. This is known as the interval value. This adjusts the distance between each trackpoint to fit the user's application. Most receivers default to some form of automatic or resolution method where a track is recorded based on the user going into a turn or traveling approximately 80 feet in a straight line. This option works best for most applications. A user-defined distance or time can also adjust the interval. Adjusting the tracks to record by distance or time may be necessary due to most receivers' limited memory to store trackpoints.

Depending on the brand and model, the storage capacity typically averages between 1,000 and 3,000 trackpoints. To extend the range of a track log, a sailboat user traveling a long distance records a trackpoint every 400 feet. A hiker on a twisty mountain trail requires more detail, so a trackpoint is recorded every 40 feet. A good distance for a road trip is 184 feet, or approximately 50 meters.

Saving Track Logs

Track logs are saved just as waypoints and routes. First, clear any previously saved unnecessary track log data. If necessary, adjust the interval value, the distance between each trackpoint, for your application. Select the Fill or Wrap option if the new track log may be longer than what the receiver can store. After the trip, select to record the track log. Most receivers will then save the track log in a reduced number of trackpoints and title the log with the current date. Like a waypoint, the log can be renamed at any time. To avoid a memory problem, users on longer-distance trips can record their travels with multiple saved track logs.

Remember the following points when saving a track log:

- Clear the track log at the starting point of the new trip.

- Save the track log at the completion of the trip.

- Be sure that the receiver is operational during the entire time of the trip. Lost satellite signals or power will result in a discontinuous log. The log will still be recorded, although broken. Nonoperational time will be recorded as a gap or a straight line between recorded tracks.

TracBack Route

Garmin has developed a TracBack feature that automatically creates
a return or inverted route with 30 waypoints from the most recently
saved track log. This feature allows you to return to the starting
position with an easy route to follow. After a track log is recorded,
simply select the TracBack option for the route conversion.

Routes

A route is a series of waypoints that are listed in the order of start to
finish. Routes may contain up to 30 or more waypoints depending on
the capacity of the receiver. Each section between two waypoints is
a leg. To create a route, select a series of waypoints in the sequence
they are to be followed.

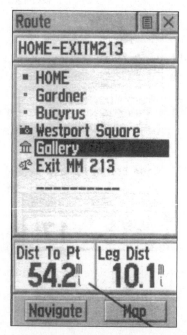

This Garmin screen shows an active route.
(Image used courtesy of Garmin Ltd. or its affiliates.
Copyright © Garmin Ltd. or its affiliates.)

Routes are beneficial because, unless you're flying or sailing, it's difficult to travel in a straight line. Obstacles require us to travel indirect paths until we reach our destination. This feature provides direction by organizing waypoints in the flow of travel. Following a route not only makes navigation easier, it also reduces the risk of error. Multiple waypoints like cabin, stand, camp, and fish, may not mean much by themselves, but when saved in a route they are given order, making an easy sequence to follow. Routes also help designate points of interest, including locations to stop for camping, eating, or refueling.

NAVIGATIONAL NUGGETS

Routes are beneficial to geocachers because they allow a series of geocaches to be saved in a sequence. Those of you who like going after multiple geocaches in the same day can be easily directed from one to the other, with the distance provided between each geocache.

Saving Routes

There are at least six ways to save routes:

- **Entered while traveling.** One of the easiest ways to create a route is by saving waypoints along the way. These waypoints are selected and added to a route.

- **Manually selected.** Previously saved waypoints are manually selected from the receiver's database in the order they are to appear in the route.

- **Loaded from a computer.** Previously recorded routes can be loaded into a receiver through the use of mapping software and a data cable.

- **From a saved track log.** Using the map pointer arrow, select key locations to save as waypoints along a track log.

- **Use the TracBack feature.** Activating this option creates a 30-waypoint route from the most recently saved track log.

- **Automatic routing.** Most newer receivers can automatically create a route to a selected location within the unit's software database. Some can even provide turn-by-turn driving directions.

When a route is saved, data is displayed on the active route page. It includes the distance between each waypoint and the total distance of the route. Detailed information is available for each leg of the trip, including the distance between waypoints, compass bearing, and ETA. Routes can also be easily edited by adding or deleting waypoints.

When a route is saved, the default name will be the date it was created. The route can be renamed at any time. One of the main benefits of using routes is that they are reversible. After the last waypoint destination is reached, the route is reversed by an Invert command to backtrack to the starting point.

Auto Routing

As GPS receivers have become more advanced, standard features include the capability to search for addresses, intersections, and businesses from a preloaded software database. Automatic routing refers to the ability of the receiver to automatically create a route to a selected location within its database.

Using a Find feature creates these automatic routes. The receiver searches for the location and then establishes a route based on user-defined criteria such as reaching the location in the fastest time, in the shortest distance, or in a direct line in an off-road mode.

Navigation gets even easier with new guidance features that provide pop-up screens and audible alarms for next-turn directions. Text screens display a directional arrow prior to each new turn in a route.

This latest technology is ideal for business travelers, emergency vehicle drivers, and anyone who needs to find unfamiliar addresses fast. These types of routing features are not always completely accurate, but they do work reasonably well. The main problem is that software is not updated fast enough to reflect street changes. Auto routing will only improve as mapping software and database points of interest continue to be updated and improved.

The Least You Need to Know

- Take the time to learn the receiver buttons and screens on your GPS. It is important to be confident when using your device for outdoor navigational use.

- Carefully go through the setup options to ensure your receiver is programmed properly.

- Learn how to enter waypoint coordinates manually. Be able to find, recall, and navigate to waypoints confidently.

- Understand track logs and routes and how they may be helpful in your outdoor use.

All About Maps

In This Chapter

- Understand the basics of map reading
- Discover why detailed topographic maps are ideal for geocaching
- Learn how to interpret the terrain through contour lines, determine distance, and navigate like a professional
- Use a map ruler to plot geocache coordinates on a topographic map
- Learn the navigation tricks and tips of the pros

At its most basic, geocaching is a matter of simply following an arrow to a destination. In the early days, this was the approach of the majority of geocachers. However, as GPS receivers have become more advanced, new tools and features, including map integration, are becoming readily available resources.

GPS users today often have at their disposal a collection of maps to help them find their ways. While most geocachers do not get into the activity as skilled map readers, many learn that understanding the basics of reading and interpreting a map can ensure that you are able to navigate with confidence.

This chapter explains map basics. You'll find out why detailed topographic (topo) maps are great for geocaching, and then you'll learn how to read them. This chapter also shows you how to determine distance in the field and how to plot GPS coordinates on a paper map. Finally, this chapter provides some navigation tips that will keep you navigating like a pro.

Map Basics

From highway to topographic, from paper to electronic formats, maps come in a number of different scales and sizes. Many GPS receivers include electronic basemaps and the ability to add maps with greater detail. It is important to have an understanding of the map options available to help ensure that you use the correct map for the job.

When viewing a paper map, check out the information along the bottom before trying to find your position in the middle. This "collar" area is full of reference information that will provide aid in reading the map. This information includes the scale, legend, distance indicators, color codes, magnetic declination, map datum, and the year the map was published. The gridlines and tick marks around the edges determine what coordinates are provided. Reviewing this information will help ensure the selection of a map in the scale and detail appropriate for your application.

Map Scales

The map *scale* is the ratio between the distance displayed on a map relative to the actual distance on the ground. The state road map kept in a glove box might be a 1:500,000 scale. Used as a highway reference, an entire state fits on one side, where 1 inch equals approximately 8 miles. When you're performing detailed ground navigation, such as when geocaching, the greater the detail the map provides, the easier it will be for you to navigate the terrain.

The primary map used for short-range detail is the 1:24,000 scale 7.5-minute topographic. In this highly detailed scale, 1 inch equals 2,000 feet. The key to choosing the right map is to choose a map that covers enough area with adequate detail to prevent you from traveling outside of its boundary.

GEO-LINGO

Maps are referred to as small or large **scale**. Small-scale maps cover a limited area in great detail. Small-scale maps range from 1:24,000 to 1:65,500. Large-scale maps are like state or highway maps that show a larger area in less detail.

Map Name Series	Scale	1 inch represents	1 centimeter represents	Map area (approximate square miles)
Puerto Rico 7.5 minute	1:20,000	1,667 feet	200 meters	71
7.5-minute	1:24,000	2,000 feet	240 meters	40 to 70
7.5- by 15-minute	1:25,000	2,083 feet	250 meters (about)	98 to 140
Alaska	1:63,360	1 mile	634 meters (about)	207 to 281
Intermediate	1:50,000	0.8 mile	500 meters (about)	County
Intermediate	1:100,000	1.6 mile	1 kilometer (about)	1,568 to 2,240
United States	1:250,000	4 miles	2. 5 kilometers (about)	4,580 to 8,669

U.S. Geological Survey map scale chart.
(U.S. Geological Survey)

Topographic Maps

In the United States, the most detailed standard map used in the backcountry is the U.S. Geological Survey (USGS) 7.5-minute topographic map. These maps can be purchased for about $4 at outdoor stores or from the USGS. They are called 7.5-minute maps because they cover 7.5 minutes of latitude and longitude. That's an area approximately 6.5 miles wide, 8.5 miles long, and 55 square miles. These maps, often referred to as *topo maps* or *topos*, provide a three-dimensional perspective of the ground. This perspective is provided using *contour lines*, which indicate terrain shape and elevation. Topographic maps also include the primary geographic coordinate systems of latitude/longitude; UTM; and township, range, and section.

GEO-LINGO

Contour lines are the curvy brown lines on a topographic map that indicate the shape of the terrain. Every fifth darker brown line is the elevation index line. This line indicates the elevation in feet or meters.

Map Reading

Map-reading skills are universally applicable, regardless of the map's scale or type. Map reading is essentially the interpretation of lines, features, landmarks, and symbols on a map. It helps to think about the map in a three-dimensional way, instead of just a flat sheet of paper. This is done by focusing on major landmarks and high and low elevation features. Contour lines on topo maps make this easier, because the lines profile the terrain.

It is helpful to maintain the "big picture" of the area in which you are traveling by keeping major landmarks in perspective. Prominent features, being man-made or natural, include all major landmarks such as mountains, highways, waterways, and bridges. Prominent features are good to use as a reference in conjunction with a map to determine your general location. Baseline features are linear reference points such as roads, rivers, and power lines. These natural boundaries are ideal to follow or use as a return point.

> **NAVIGATIONAL NUGGETS**
>
> When geocaching, it is wise to bring a paper map and compass in addition to your GPS receiver. In this way, you can get to the geocache by the most appropriate means, while ensuring your safe return in the case that your GPS receiver fails.

In the field, maps are easier to read if they are set to the terrain, matching the prominent and baseline features on the map with those on the ground. This is known as *terrain association*. This helps reference landmarks and gives the user a better understanding of what lies ahead. This is done with the assistance of a compass by rotating the map until the top faces true north.

Understanding how to read topographic maps is important when tackling tough terrain outdoors.
(Chris Ratelle)

Reading Topographic Maps

Our example is a 7.5-minute topo map of the Bohemia mining district, south of Cottage Grove, Oregon. This map was located by reviewing a state of Oregon USGS map coverage index to find the map of our exact area of interest. The state index map is divided into titled 7.5-minute sections. Our map is titled Fairview Peak Quadrangle-Oregon. The bottom section of the map gives details that include the following:

- **Map date.** Produced in 1986, revised in 1997. Topographic information is from 1980.

- **Datum.** North American Datum of 1927 (NAD 27). The datum is the global survey system used to create the map. This is important because GPS receivers need to be programmed to the same datum used to create the map.

- **Declination diagram.** The scale indicating the degree a compass is adjusted to correct magnetic north to true north. This map's declination is 17.5° as of 1999.

- **Map scale.** 1:24,000; 1 inch equals 24,000 inches on the ground.

- **Mileage scale.** One mile equals about 2 ⁵/₈ inches.

- **Contour interval.** The elevation lines are 40 feet apart, every fifth darker brown line indicates the elevation in feet.

- **Other information.** This includes where this map is located in relation to the state, map names surrounding this map, and a list of symbols for highways and roads.

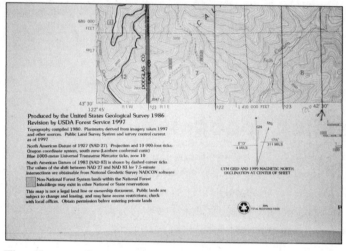

The collar area of a topographic map provides the information you need to read the map accurately.

(Jack W. Peters)

Check the Datum

When using GPS with any map, be sure to program the GPS receiver to the correct datum used on the map. Many U.S. topo maps use North American Datum 1927 (NAD 27 CONUS), or possibly the datum used in geocaching, World Geodetic System 1984 (WGS 84). In Europe, it is the Ordnance Survey Great Britain (OSGB).

The receiver is set to a default datum: Check the Setup menu to ensure it is the correct one for your application. Failing to make this adjustment can cause errors of as much as 1,000 meters.

Grid Lock

Notice from the corner of this topo map that there are tick marks, lines, and numbers everywhere. Besides latitude/longitude and UTM coordinates, there are grids to indicate township, range, and section. To confuse matters further, there are also six-digit numbers with "FEET" behind them. This is a State Plane Coordinate (SPC) system, which is similar to UTM but uses feet rather than meters. When referencing numbers and tick marks, be sure you are referencing the correct markings before taking any readings.

Map Colors and Symbols

Topo maps are color-coded and are covered with symbols and markings. Fortunately, most are relatively self-explanatory. For example, on the color codes, black is used to designate roads, buildings, and other man-made objects. Blue is used to designate waterways, and brown is used for the contour lines. For a complete list of map symbols, check with the U.S. Geological Survey or whoever produces your favorite paper maps.

Contour Lines

Contour lines show the map's topography by indicating the shape of the terrain and its elevation. These lines make it possible to determine the height of the terrain and the depths of bodies of water. These lines do not cross each other because they join points of equal elevation. Every fifth line is darker and is known as an index line. The index lines provide the specific elevation listed in feet or meters above sea level. On our example topo, the elevation is listed in feet. There is a distance of 40 feet between each line, equaling 200 feet between each index line. The amount of distance between each line is known as the contour interval.

DEAD BATTERIES

Be aware that maps can be inaccurate, even detailed topos. The data can be outdated and errors are sometimes made during the interpretation of the aerial photographs. Not surprisingly, locations on the ground often look entirely different from what you might think they would look like from a map.

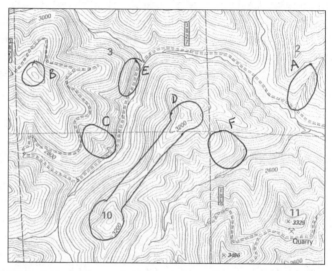

Each topographic map contour line represents a change in elevation. On most 7.5-minute maps this elevation measurement is 40 feet. Remember that contour lines may not indicate cliffs or crevasses that will make travel difficult.
(Jack W. Peters)

Contour lines provide a low-tech way for a map to come alive by providing a three-dimensional view of the terrain. Reading these lines is simple: the closer the lines are together, the steeper the terrain. Open-spaced contoured areas are flat; heavily lined areas are steep or cliff walls. With V-shaped contours, the tip of the V points uphill, as seen with creeks and rivers. U-shaped contours typically point downhill. The following are typical terrain features:

A. V-shaped lines point to upriver. In this example, a creek is flowing down into a larger river.

B. Mountain peak, indicated by the way the interval between circular contour lines becomes narrower toward the top.

C. Spurs, most likely caused by an ancient creek.

D. Saddle, where a plateau joins two mountain peaks.

E. Cliff wall, as indicated by a concentration of contour lines.

F. U-shaped lines point downhill.

Pacing

Some geocaches and GPS challenges require the ability to measure distance in the field. Pacing is a reasonably accurate way to do so by knowing the distance of your stride. A "stride" is two steps, the distance between where the same foot hits the ground twice. Tally strides by counting every time the same foot hits the ground.

To use this system, you have to know the distance of your stride. To determine the distance of your stride, measure off a predetermined distance, such as 100 feet, or 50 meters, and count the number of strides it takes to cover that distance.

Here are some points to consider while pacing:

- One stride (two steps) equals approximately 60 inches or 5 feet.

- Know how many of your strides are in 100 feet or 50 meters, whichever sys-tem is used.

- Each person's stride varies with his own height and the terrain.

- Compensate for travel conditions that shorten strides (for instance, weather, mud, snow, wind, visibility, and backpacks).

NAVIGATIONAL NUGGETS

Keeping track of pacing distances is easier with the aid of "pace beads" or handheld punch counters. Pace beads are used by sliding a bead over a string after a set number of paces. These aids reduce the chance for error and allow you to concentrate on counting paces instead of trying to remember distances.

Plotting GPS Coordinates

Have you ever thought of how great it would be to transfer geocache coordinates from a GPS receiver to a paper topographic map? Well, it is possible through the use of a map ruler. This calculation is easily done through mapping software that automatically provides the coordinates wherever a cursor is placed on a map. With paper maps, however, it requires the ability to measure the target's location with a special map ruler.

NAVIGATIONAL NUGGETS

Using a map ruler will allow you to transfer coordinates from a map to a GPS receiver. Coordinates can be measured from a map and then entered as a waypoint into a receiver, or a waypoint from a receiver can be plotted on a map.

With a little practice, waypoint locations can be plotted on a map, or the coordinates can be obtained for a location of interest on a map. If you can master this skill, you will have reached a pinnacle of ability in map and GPS use. The ability to know your location on a paper map provides you with real freedom to travel while keeping your location and the surrounding landmarks in perspective. For geocachers, this is a great tool for plotting groups of geocaches on a detailed topo map.

Map rulers are available to measure both latitude/longitude and UTM coordinates. Using either system requires preparing the map by using a long ruler to connect the geographic coordinate tick marks. Turn the map into a grid by connecting the tick marks from side to side and top to bottom. USGS 7.5-minute maps include both the latitude/longitude and UTM system. For latitude/longitude, there are two tick marks on each side of the map every 2.5 minutes apart. Connecting these creates a nine-section grid that resembles a tick-tack-toe board. These maps are approximately 10 kilometers wide and 14 kilometers long. Connecting the blue UTM tick marks creates 140, 1,000-meter or 1-kilometer sections.

The grid lines represent a known coordinate location. A map ruler measures the distance between the known location at the grid line to the target. This is where the UTM system really shines through. Finding a location within a 1,000-meter section is much easier than trying to find a location with degrees, minutes, and seconds. This is because UTM grids are square, representing 1,000 meters or 1 kilometer in height and width. To find the coordinates, it's just a matter of counting meters east and north to the target.

Measuring latitude/longitude is a little trickier because these grids are not square. Remember, grid lines are compressed as they get closer to the North and South Poles. This factor, except at the Equator, makes the grids rectangular. Measurements are still easy to do, but taking the longitude reading requires an extra step. Here's a rundown on taking measurements with each coordinate system.

UTM System

Using the UTM system is the way to go for detailed ground-work. One simple measurement will get you the coordinates within a few meters of accuracy. Here are the steps involved in taking a measurement:

1. Grid the map by connecting the UTM tick marks, creating 1-kilometer sections.

2. Find the grid section that contains the target.

3. Use a map ruler UTM scale that matches the map you are using. Placing the beginning end of the ruler on the grid line, take a measurement from left to right to the target. You are measuring east for the Easting coordinate.

4. Determine the number of meters from the grid line to the target and write them down. Next take a measurement from the bottom grid line and measure north for the Northing coordinate. Determine the meters and write them down. Now simply add the Easting and Northing meters to the baseline coordinates.

When plotting coordinates on a map, you follow the same procedure. Mark the map where the Easting and Northing numbers come together to find the target.

In the following example, a measurement is taken of the Puddin Rock Road staging area.

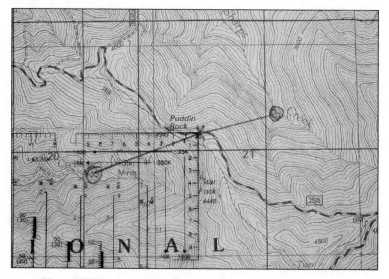

Using UTM, one quick measurement provides both Easting and Northing coordinates.
(Jack W. Peters)

Remember, the UTM coordinates increase from bottom to top and from left to right. The target is in the grid of 524 and 525 Easting, and 4823 and 4824 Northing. The ruler is used to measure the number of meters from the baseline to the target.

Easting is the first measurement. The number increases from left to right. Measure from the left grid line 524; the target is an additional 480 meters. Add the number for the coordinate of 524480 E.

The next measurement is Northing. The target is about 127 meters north of the 4823 baseline. Adding the meters provides the coordinate of 4823127 N.

Latitude/Longitude System

Map rulers are available to measure latitude/longitude in the full address of degrees, minutes, and seconds or in decimal minutes. In this example, we will be measuring in degrees, minutes, and seconds. Here are the steps to take a measurement:

1. Grid the map by connecting the tick marks every 2.5 minutes apart, creating nine, 2.5-minute sections.

2. Find the grid section that contains the target.

3. Use a map ruler scale that matches the scale of your map. The first measurement is north/south measurement of latitude. From the grid line below the target, measure straight up counting the minutes and seconds to the target.

4. Finding longitude is a different procedure because the distance between these grid lines decreases as they become closer to the North and South Poles. This requires placing the beginning of the ruler at the lower right corner of the grid section. Bring the other side of the ruler up and over to the opposing grid line to the left of the target. The ruler will be at approximately a 45-degree angle.

5. Slide the ruler up until the target intersects with the ruler. When taking a measurement, be sure that both ends of the ruler are touching the dividing grid lines.

6. Measure the minutes and seconds from the lower right corner to the target, and then add the distance to the longitude baseline.

To plot coordinates on a map, you follow the same procedure. Mark the map where the latitude and longitude coordinates come together. The intersecting lines mark the target.

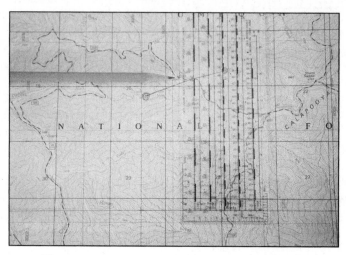

Measure minutes and seconds up from the base grid line.
(Jack W. Peters)

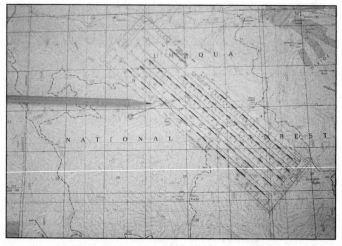

Measure minutes and seconds over from the east base grid line at an angle
(because of the compression of longitude lines).
(Jack W. Peters)

The 2.5-minute × 2.5-minute section the target is located in is north of 32' 30" latitude, and to the west of 40' longitude. The first measurement is latitude. Remember, latitude numbers increase from south to north. We've started the ruler on the 32' 30" baseline. The minutes and seconds up to the target are 1 minute and 15 seconds. Now add the distance to the latitude baseline of 32' 30". The latitude is 43° 33' 45".

In finding longitude, place the beginning end of the ruler at the lower right corner (the 40' line). Bring the other side of the ruler up and over to match the vertical dividing line to the left of the target (the 42' 30" line). Remember, longitude increases from east to west.

Place each end of the ruler on the vertical grid lines, at approximately a 45-degree angle. Slide the ruler up until the target intersects with the ruler. The minutes and seconds over to the target are 1 minute and 50 seconds. Add this distance to the 40' baseline. The longitude is 122° 41' 50".

Navigation Tips

Combining the traditional map and compass skills with a few tips will have you navigating like a professional. Understanding these skills also enables you to use your GPS receiver to its fullest potential. Here's a list of useful navigational skills to help keep you on track.

- **Aiming off.** This is traveling on a compass bearing in an indirect path to your target. This is done to bypass an obstacle, or to help find a target on a linear feature. For example, you believe your truck is parked on a roadway straight ahead at about 5°. You cannot see the vehicle because of dense vegetation, so you aim off slightly to the right at 15° knowing that when you reach the roadway, the truck will be to your left.

- **Calculate map distances.** Keep a small piece of wire in your navigation kit for measuring distances on a map. Bend the wire to follow a road or trail, and then straighten it out to find the distance using the map scale.

- **Catch features.** These are features that indicate that you have missed a turn or have traveled too far. If circumstances make a destination difficult to find, know what roads or features are beyond the location. That way you will know whether you have traveled too far when you reach the catch feature you have chosen.

- **Confirm location by elevation.** Altimeters are a useful way to help confirm your location on a map. Compare altimeter elevation readings with map markings. Remember, a GPS receiver's altimeter may not be as accurate as a manual barometric altimeter.

- **Dead reckoning.** This is used to confirm your location by recording your travels from a last known position. It requires keeping track of every distance and bearing traveled. Starting from a known position, record your route on a map or in a journal. This is an ideal way to back up a GPS receiver when traveling in unknown territory.

- **Directions from nature.** Remember the basics: the sun rises in the east, moves to the south, and then sets in the west. At night, find the North Star; also, the points on a crest moon point south.

- **Night navigation.** When traveling in darkness, remember that our natural night vision takes about 30 minutes to fully develop. Red LED lights or flashlight filters work great for producing adequate light without losing night vision. Besides using GPS, keep track of time and use pacing to maintain your position. Remember, pacing steps will be considerably shorter at night, and be sure that your compass glows in the dark.

- **Reverse perspective.** While traveling, remember to turn around and look for the reverse perspective. This is what the road or trail will look like when you return. Every few minutes, take a 360-degree scan. Notice the scenery and landmarks in every direction, paying special attention to what it looks like behind you.

- **Trail markers.** Manually back up your track log the old-fashioned way with the use of trail markers. Use natural resources, such as placing rocks or drawing arrows in the dirt with a stick.

- **Triangulation.** You learned how to use triangulation to confirm the location of a geocache. In this application, your location can be confirmed by taking a bearing to at least two or more different surrounding landmarks. A current location is determined by plotting the intersection of the bearings on a map.

The Least You Need to Know

- Various map options are available to ensure that you use the correct map when geocaching.

- Pay attention to important collar information and the coordinate system used on your topographic map.

- On most 7.5-minute topographic maps, each contour line indicates a change in elevation by 40 feet.

- Pacing is a remarkably accurate way to measure distances in the field by counting your stride. A stride is two complete and normal steps.

- You can use a map ruler to plot geocaches on a paper topographic map.

- When geocaching or hiking, traditional map and compass navigational skills enhance the use of GPS receiver, and will be critical if your electronic gear fails.

Computers and Software

In This Chapter

- Explore how you can use computers to save, transfer, and organize your data
- Get the hang of tracking your current location on computer mapping software
- Learn how to make GPS receivers and computers work together
- Find out about the latest programs available to enhance your geocaching experience
- Discover developments in geocaching with GPS-enabled phones

If you're already geocaching, you likely know how to use a computer. However, you may not be aware of just how well computers and GPS devices work together. Through the use of map software programs and GPS devices, computers can be highly useful navigational tools. Whether at home or in the field, you can plan your trip by studying where you're going and how to get there. When you get back home, you can save a log of your travels and even share it with your friends.

This chapter explains how to utilize desktop and mobile computers in GPS and navigation, including how to manage, transfer, and save data for your geocaching adventures.

GPS with Computers

GPS and computers go together as naturally as geocaching and adventure. There are many applications for using computers in navigation, with or without a GPS device. Computers can run highly detailed mapping software and can even be transformed into GPS receivers. Desktop computers work great for trip planning, whereas laptops and handheld PDAs are more easily taken into the field for more versatility.

Computers are used as a tool for navigation in four ways: as a receiver, as a map database, for data transfer and management, and for real-time tracking.

EUREKA!

To use a GPS receiver with other electronic devices, purchase one with a data port compatible with National Marine Electronics Association (NMEA) protocols. The NMEA has established a universal electronic standard to allow compatibility between GPS receivers and other electronic gear.

Computers as GPS Receivers

Laptop and handheld computers are easily converted into GPS receivers through kits that include software and a remote antenna. Laptops with built-in Bluetooth support can also use Bluetooth-enabled GPS devices. The advantage of doing so includes the ability to use computer equipment you already own and carry it with you. Computers have large color screens and virtually unlimited memory compared to GPS receivers. In addition, a greater number of higher-quality map programs are available for computers as opposed to GPS devices.

It might be possible to save a little money by not duplicating gear. Keep in mind, however, that laptop and PDA setups do not have nearly the durability of a standard GPS receiver. Moisture and vibration can quickly disable the electronics. Computer-based setups are best for vehicle-based applications due to high power consumption and limited durability.

EUREKA!

Protective case manufacturers such as Pelican make special water- and shockproof cases to protect PDAs, cell phones, and other electronic gear.

Map Databases

One of the benefits of having a computer along is that any one CD, DVD, or SD card can store more map data than your glove box could ever dream. Any of these resources can include highly detailed data on a favorite region or general highway map information for a whole country. The convenience of having highway, regional, and topographic maps in such a compact format is great. Plus, you don't have to fold them!

Despite the convenience of computer maps, they will not altogether replace paper maps, especially when hiking outdoors. Paper maps have a time and place for use and can be easier to read while bouncing down the road or identifying your location while out on the trail.

Data Transfer and Management

For geocaching, mobile computers work great for storing downloaded geocache data. Really, you can never have too many geocaches available for you to find! Computer-based mapping software is ideal when managing navigation data and for trip planning. Before heading outdoors, make sure to review the locations on a map. Geocache locations and other points of interest can be easily analyzed to help determine where to go and how to get there.

Besides creating and storing information, data can be transferred between computers and GPS receivers. Placing waypoints and route data created by trip-planning software on your receiver is incredibly helpful. Not only does it save considerable time but it also reduces the risk of error from manually entering coordinates or other information in the field. Upon your return, waypoints, tracks, and route data saved using your GPS receiver can also be transferred back to your computer to help document your travels!

Another benefit of this feature is the ability to share GPS data with a friend. Waypoints for your favorite geocaches and outdoor areas can be easily saved and transferred. Plug a friend's GPS receiver into your computer and he can follow in your footsteps.

Real-Time Tracking

Real-time tracking is a fascinating way to use your receiver. An icon of your location appears in the center of the digital map and displays your movements on the computer screen. Your position normally remains in the center of the screen while the map moves as you travel.

GPS track logs are helpful when logging your geocaching adventures. They also help ensure your safe return.

(Carleen Pruess)

Displaying your location and direction of travel on a larger computer screen, rather than a small-screen receiver, is helpful if you are using a receiver without a basemap. It also provides two different screens of data. The driver can monitor the GPS receiver for information like speed and compass bearing, while the passenger watches your position on the computer.

To set up this feature, plug your GPS receiver's data cable into an open port on a laptop or PDA. After the hardware is connected, settings are required in the receiver and computer mapping software to allow GPS track-log data to be transferred to the computer program. Most map software will support real-time tracking.

Setup menu options in both the GPS receivers and map software programs provide various interface options. The primary interface for real-time tracking and other receiver/computer functions is NMEA mode. As previously mentioned, the NMEA established this mode for electronic and navigation product compatibility. In the map software program, be sure to select the correct data port used for the data transfer. The next setup option is the baud rate. This is the rate at which electronic data is sent. The primary baud rate for real-time tracking is 4800. An incorrect baud rate is one of the primary reasons for interface failure. It may take a little experimenting to get the right settings, but it's worth the effort when you see your location appear on the computer screen.

DEAD BATTERIES

When driving, computers, cell phones, and GPS receivers can grow beyond distractions to serious hazards. Don't let the use of this gear get you into an accident. Let your passenger manage the electronics while you keep your eyes on the road.

Mapping Software

Mapping software is available in a variety of applications from many sources. It is a very practical application that provides tools and resources that geocachers often consider invaluable.

The following are examples of standard features found in most mapping software applications:

- **Creating waypoints and routes.** Moving a cursor on a map program instantly provides coordinate information based on the cursor's location on the map. Waypoints are created with a simple click of a mouse. Routes are easily created after waypoints are saved. Waypoints appear on the map and can be customized with names, colors, and symbols.

- **Real-time tracking.** Using a GPS receiver to transfer a live track log into computer mapping software.

- **Recording travel history.** Track logs recorded in the field can be transferred back to a computer and saved as a recorded history of your travels. Computers provide virtually unlimited storage compared to the limited memory available in most receivers.

- **Search feature.** Most map programs provide a search feature allowing parks, towns, and other landmarks to be found instantly.

- **Terrain analysis.** Moving a cursor over a map instantly provides elevation. Connecting two points instantly provides an elevation profile, distance, or bearing.

- **Transferring waypoints, routes, and track logs.** Through the use of a data cable, data can be transferred back and forth between a GPS receiver and a computer.

The following subsections provide explanations of some of the types of map software available.

GPS Company Software

GPS manufacturers provide proprietary mapping software that works exclusively with their brands of GPS receivers. Additional map detail can be purchased on CD, DVD, or SD card to enhance a device's own basemap. For example, topographic, city, or nautical information can be purchased to improve navigation and enhance your receiver use. Imagine trying to navigate to a geocache without street names or trail data! Map software is typically available for major cities, regional areas, various countries, and other parts of the world.

Besides upgrading a receiver's basemap, the latest software programs include commercial metro or travel information such as the location of restaurants, hotels, gas stations, and other helpful points of interest.

Aftermarket Software

Traditional map manufacturers like DeLorme and National Geographic also provide electronic maps for use with computers and PDA devices. These programs work great for planning trips as well as for creating, transferring, and saving travel data. They include a number of neat features, such as the ability to convert trails and roads into routes, and can provide a 3-D display of your map data. They cannot, however, be used to enhance a GPS receiver's existing basemap.

The U.S. Geological Survey offers digital maps known as digital raster graphics (DRG). DRGs are standard topographic maps scanned and made available in an electronic TIFF file. A 7.5-minute DRG averages 8 megabytes. These maps can be combined with other digital media, such as photographic or satellite data, for a unique perspective.

Map companies offer large topographic maps with your favorite location in the center. This is helpful in avoiding the problem of hiking into a map's corner, or having to bring multiple maps because the subject area is on the boundary. These maps can include any coordinate grid lines desired, and most are printed on waterproof paper. Map kiosk centers are becoming popular in outdoor stores. These centers are capable of instantly printing topographic maps of your favorite areas.

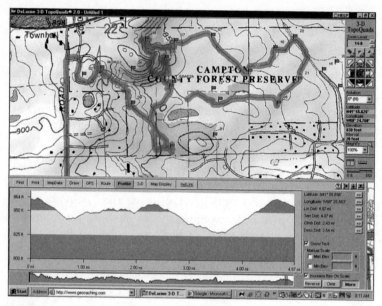

Using DeLorme software, the map shows a track log and waypoints from an event in St. Charles, Illinois.

(DeLorme)

Online Map Services

Online map services like Google Maps enable you to instantly conduct an Internet search to obtain a map of any area of interest. Depending on your preferred map site, you can enter coordinates to locations and then create and print a route or map with the location clearly marked.

When preparing to go geocaching, remember that many of these map services are available on the Geocaching.com cache details page. It's easy to select and view a map of the geocache online. On Geocaching.com, you can also use Google Maps to filter geocache types in real-time as you view and drag the map online.

Most online mapping services are free and can be very helpful in providing quick and accurate mapping information.

EUREKA!

You can use aerial photography similar to what intelligence agencies have been using for years. Geocache information pages on Geocaching. com include links to a variety of maps, including those featuring aerial photography.

Terrain Analysis

One of the primary benefits of using digital maps is the ability to study terrain. Regardless of software type, most applications provide features to allow you to study the ground before you get there. Knowing such factors as elevation and slope will make it easier to plan your trip. Determining how steep trails and roads are may make a difference in whether you can hike or drive there, or even help you determine whether you can bring children along for the hike.

Selecting two points with a click of a mouse can immediately provide distance bearing or elevation profiling. Maptech's Terrain Navigator software provides a unique 3-D perspective of any selected area. In 3-D mode, the area map can be rotated, tilted, and viewed from any bearing or elevation. A selected area can also be viewed in a topo map or aerial photo view format.

In the preceding example, a group of caches are profiled in the Mount Pisgah area. The cache locations were entered and then Maptech's 3-D mode was activated to analyze the surrounding terrain. These high-tech tools are excellent for making flat maps come alive and making them much easier to interpret. Studying this information is as interesting as it is practical. Knowing what to expect can help avoid errors in calculating travel time and difficulty.

EUREKA!

Check your GPS receiver's manufacturer's website to determine the latest version of operating software or firmware that is available for your receiver. Manufacturers often update this software to fix bugs and make other improvements. Most receivers can be easily upgraded through an online download. There is typically no cost, and it takes only a few minutes.

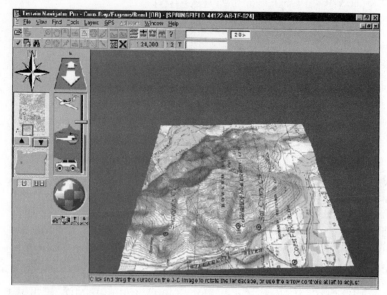

Electronic maps, such as this example from Maptech, provide many helpful features, including three-dimensional viewing.

(Maptech)

Taking Computers Geocaching

Laptop computers may be a little bulky to pack on a geocaching road trip, but they are definitely getting smaller and faster. They also have the power to manage your serious geocache adventures.

The following sections outline some practical ways to use a portable computer outdoors.

Load Lots of Maps

Most computers provide enough storage to load a number of mapping software programs. This capability provides a useful variety of mapping options, ranging from detailed topographic maps to street and trip planning. This software allows you to trade those badly folded paper maps in the glove box (but don't throw them out yet) for an often quicker way to find the best access to the next geocache.

Geocaches by the Thousand!

Once you decide on the area in which you want to go geocaching, you can request a Pocket Query from Geocaching.com. A Pocket Query provides the ability to create custom searches so that you can receive information on only the caches you want to search for. At any time, you may have several hundred geocaches stored on your computer with waypoints and details for each geocache that are waiting to be found.

The information included in a Pocket Query is typically imported into a mapping software program for easy viewing of the geocaches. The cache locations are shown on detailed maps, making it easy to visually see the locations of geocaches in relationship to each other. Some newer models of GPS receivers allow you to import GPX files directly using a data cable.

Ready to head outdoors? Simply use a GPS data-transfer program to download the waypoint data from your computer into your GPS receiver, and you are set. It may sound like a complicated process, but once you've done this a few times you will feel like a pro.

Time for Real-Time Tracking

Finding your "live" location on mapping computer software is as easy as connecting your GPS receiver to your computer with a data cable and selecting the correct GPS and computer settings for real-time tracking. Real-time tracking is great for indicating your exact location in relation to all of the caches you want to find. It also helps select which roads to take and where to turn to find each cache more efficiently. Using the receiver's GOTO feature indicates how far you are from each cache you want to find. Having all of this data allows you to more easily plan the order in which you'll search for the caches.

Geocaching Software to Enhance Your Game

Because geocaching was adopted early on by computer and gadget geeks, those players began developing applications to improve their game from the start. Many of the programs that geocachers use today can be traced to the pioneers of the activity who contributed their time and know-how to their favorite activity. Other tools began as programs to enhance GPS usage and developed geocaching-specific functions as players adopted them for their own use.

It is difficult to say which programs are essential to geocaching. What *is* essential is finding something that works for you and gets you outside a little faster. A list of a few of the programs commonly used by geocachers follows:

- **GSAK (Geocaching Swiss Army Knife).** This is an all-in-one tool for managing your activity as a geocacher. GSAK enables you to load Geocaching.com Pocket Queries onto your computer and export them directly to your GPS or PDA. Chances are you'll never exhaust all the features of this program, but you'll have fun trying.

- **EasyGPS.** You just can't beat the price of EasyGPS—it's free! EasyGPS works with every popular handheld GPS device and can transfer waypoints, track logs, and routes from your computer to GPS and vise versa. EasyGPS is great for backing up the information on your GPS and saving it for future use.

- **Google Earth.** Google Earth's interactive features make exploring maps fun. The detailed images available make it a much more personal experience than simply staring at a map. Pocket Query data can be loaded into Google Earth for viewing geocache locations and even following the travels of Travel Bugs and other trackables.

- **CacheMate.** This program has been around for several years and has managed to grow a lot in that time. CacheMate is a program for viewing Pocket Query information on a handheld PDA. In addition, notes can be taken through CacheMate and used later to write online logs. CacheMate was initially available only for Palm devices but has expanded for Pocket PC as well.

Groundspeak Pocket Query as displayed using Google Earth.

Geocaching by Phone

With today's GPS-enabled phones you can find yourself geocaching without ever having to break out your old trusty GPS device. In fact, you won't even need to log on to your home computer to download the geocache locations or log your finds afterwards. All these steps can be accomplished through the use of your GPS-enabled phone.

The Trimble Geocache Navigator

The Trimble Geocache Navigator is a fully featured geocaching application for mobile phones. The software combines the GPS that is built into your phone with your phone's wireless data network to allow you to search for caches near your current location, address, coordinates, or waypoint.

You can then navigate to the geocache by following the arrow on your phone's screen, just as you would with your GPS. Once you find the cache, you can log your find right from your phone. Learn more at www.trimbleoutdoors.com.

Groundspeak's Geocaching iPhone Application

As the anticipation built over the release of the GPS-enabled iPhone 3G, geocachers began wondering what would be in store for their favorite game. Groundspeak answered with this all-in-one application that puts the geocaching world in the palm of your hand.

The iPhone 3G uses a combination of GPS, Wi-Fi positioning, and cell towers to determine your approximate location. Groundspeak's iPhone Application then queries the Geocaching.com database in real-time and provides a list of geocaches near you. The application can also geocode addresses, search using a location from your address book, or look up a geocache by it's GC code.

On your iPhone, simply open the application, select a geocache you want to search for, hit the "navigate" button, and follow the arrow on your iPhone screen. You can also access the geocache details including recent logs and hints. You can even access the trackables pages to find out goals of Travel Bugs and geocoins while out on the trail.

As the mobile computing world continues to grow, geocaching seems determined to grow with it. New GPS-enabled devices simply means more opportunity for more geocachers to get out and have fun.

Groundspeak's Geocaching iPhone Application provides similar functionality to Geocaching.com, making it easy to navigate.
(Groundspeak)

Geocache search results page as shown using Groundspeak's
Geocaching iPhone Application.
(Groundspeak)

Some Final Computer Bytes

With all this technology and the trip-planning features of mapping software, there is no doubt that bringing along a computer will allow you to get around much faster and more efficiently. It will also enable you to find more geocaches than you could have ever done before.

Remember that electronics do not hold up well to abuse. Vibration and moisture can easily send your expensive gear on a one-way ticket to the service shop. Also, remember that thieves often target computer and electronic gear so be sure to secure them and keep them out of sight when out on the trail.

EUREKA!

Some computer manufacturers make gear for extreme outdoor use, like the military-grade Panasonic Toughbook.

You must remember to use caution and not allow these electronics to become a dangerous distraction. Regardless of how you're traveling, taking your eyes off the road for a second to watch a screen can result in a serious accident. Allow a passenger to run the GPS and other gear so you can concentrate on driving, or pull over to do it yourself.

The Least You Need to Know

- If needed, you can easily convert your portable computer into a GPS receiver.
- The NMEA electronic format enables you to use your receiver with other gear including computers, cameras, and radios, so make sure to look for NMEA compatibility with any equipment you buy.
- Using computer mapping software will allow you to easily manage waypoints, routes, and track logs.
- There is a wide variety of geocaching software available to help you better organize your geocaching trips.
- GPS-enabled phones and other devices are becoming increasingly available for geocaching.

Welcome to the Community

By now you're out there finding geocaches with the best of them. Each Travel Bug you release goes on journeys more epic than a Cecil B. DeMille movie, and you can read a map better than you can read your own handwriting. So what's left? If you're ready to advance to the next level, Part 4 is for you.

Get acquainted with the geocaching community: fun-loving, family-oriented, outdoor enthusiasts like yourself. Geocachers get together and find geocaches in nearly every country in the world. Discover how you can set up your own geocaching group and how you can take your favorite activity on vacation. Learn about attending or hosting one of the many geocaching events held around the world!

Geocaching Groups, Forums, and Events

In This Chapter

- Online interactions and community building
- Local geocaching clubs and organizations
- Event caches that bring geocachers together
- Organizing your own event

When you think of geocaching, an image might come to mind of one or two people out by themselves on a trail. In certain cases, that is true. Geocaching is a great way to get away from it all and simply enjoy nature. Yet, as the activity evolved, geocaching quickly became one driven by social interaction. For many people, geocaching is not only a way to spend quality time with family and friends but also a way to share similar experiences and meet new people.

Chances are, when you started geocaching you didn't know any other players. As you became more involved, you slowly got to know other geocachers through their logs, the geocaches they placed, forum posts, and the occasional e-mail exchange. What often develops out of those first geocaching interactions are friendships that run deeper than the game itself. You can find people who share a lot of the same interests and create relationships that feel like family—complete with that crazy uncle that no one quite seems to understand.

Geocachers are an international group of fun-loving people made up of every age, sex, race, and background. Most geocachers will agree that the next best thing to finding a well-hidden geocache is sharing the adventure with other geocachers.

It's great fun to meet other geocachers, whether online, on the trail, or at one of the many geocaching events. It is especially enjoyable the first time you get to associate a face and personality to the geocaching username of someone you've met online. You will probably find that many geocachers are not too different from you. Many geocachers have busy lives with family, children, and careers. But in all of life's chaos, they take the time to seek out a geocache or two, and they also take time to get together with each other to share the many experiences of geocaching.

Since the inception of the activity, many geocachers have established friendships, teams, groups, and organizations; these enable them to get even more enjoyment from geocaching. Some have even found love through geocaching and proposed marriage using a specially placed geocache! Geocachers spend hours online and off discussing all aspects of geocaching, from rules and policy to adventures and experiences.

In this chapter, you'll learn how geocachers use online forums, local organizations, and events to cultivate an active social community.

A milestone geocache for The RidgeRunners.
(Peter Durrant)

Online Interactions

The Internet was a key element in the development of geocaching and has been equally responsible for its rapid growth. The web is used in a number of ways, ranging from informing new players about the activity and listing the available geocaches to allowing geocachers to keep in contact and discuss their favorite hobby. The following sections discuss some of these online groups and forums.

Geocaching.com Discussion Forums

Groundspeak's online forum has been a key element in the development of geocaching. The online discussion forum provides a setting where any geocacher can ask questions or search for answers. These discussion forums start off with someone asking a question or making an announcement or comment. Then, others respond and the conversation continues in the form of a discussion thread. A discussion thread is the topic that ties a string of conversations together.

The forum has dedicated areas of topic discussion that range from "Getting Started," an area for newbies, to technical forums like "GPS and Technology," where geocachers can seek product reviews and information. There are also unique content areas, including an area dedicated to "The Hunt/The Unusual" for sharing your own bizarre and fascinating geocaching stories.

These forums are filled with geocaching's colorful characters, many of whom are the pioneers of the activity and who helped it evolve into what it is today. Geocaching continues to evolve because of participants like you who test the latest GPS gear or Geocaching.com site changes and who consistently contribute new ideas. But we warn you, it's easy to get lost for hours in the ongoing discussions, learning and chatting about everything you ever wondered about geocaching!

After a little while in the forums, you will begin to become familiar with the personalities of many of the geocachers who post and participate frequently. If you have a question and post it in the discussion forums, you will likely receive your answer within minutes, or you might get *markwelled*.

> **GEO-LINGO**
>
> Often in the Geocaching.com discussion forums, you may be **markwelled** when you ask a question. "Markwelling" is a geocaching term that refers to when someone points you to a discussion in the past that answers your current question. Markwelling originates from geocacher Markwell, who would often direct new geocachers to existing topics.

The Geocaching.com forums are a great place to learn about the latest developments in the GPS-based gaming circles, such as new product releases, fixes, contests, and a variety of other topics related to geocaching. With millions of posts and a searchable format, the geocaching forums are a great place to start for those with a lot of questions or a hunger to expand their knowledge of geocaching.

Regional and Local Forums and Websites

Within the Groundspeak forums you will find a host of regional forums that cover just about every area around the globe. These forums are great places to discuss geocaching in the local environment, focusing on specific issues and details that would not be as pertinent to a broader forum. These are also great places to get to know some of the geocachers in your home area. Some of the regional forum discussions take place in that specific region's native language.

Discussions about geocaching on a local level often take on some very important topics. Issues of how to promote geocaching in a specific area or working with local park boards are best discussed in these types of forums. Aside from the Groundspeak regional forums you can also find a wide variety of local geocaching clubs and organizations that have their own websites and discussion groups for just these purposes.

Online Sharing for the Masses

Just as geocaching has evolved, so too have the number of ways in which people can share their beloved activity. There are hosted podcasts from around the world in addition to thousands of personal blogs, photos, and videos dedicated to geocaching adventures. A simple online search of "geocaching" can return many hours of enjoyment, reading about and learning of adventures from around the world!

Local Clubs and Geocaching Organizations

Ready to get more involved? Want to meet local geocachers on a more frequent basis or do you have a strong desire to give back to your local community? Join or create a local geocaching club or organization.

You can often find links to local geocaching organizations within the Groundspeak regional forums. If not, you can ask some of the more established geocachers in the area. Chances are they're familiar with the different websites, e-mail groups, or forums that exist in the area.

Many of the more established geocaching organizations have developed their own websites and resources, and represent regional or metro areas, so they're helpful in keeping members informed about the latest news and events in their areas. These organizations help new geocachers by providing the basic information to get started, building a local geocaching identity, hosting and promoting events, and helping to facilitate relationships with local land managers.

So there are active geocachers in your area but no established club or organization? This might be the ideal time to start your own organization. Being part of a local group is a great way to meet fellow geocachers as well as get out more often by planning events and outings. An organization also enables you to promote the activity and provide a positive public image through projects such as trail maintenance or Cache In Trash Out (CITO) events. These are discussed in more detail later in this chapter.

The first step is to get the locals together. An easy way to do this is by hosting an event cache. This is a cache where participants find a social event instead of a cache container. Find a family-friendly park or pizza parlor, record the coordinates, and post the event on Geocaching.com. Event caches are also covered in more detail later in this chapter.

Publicize the event by posting notices in local, regional, and Geocaching.com discussion forums, and send invitations to people finding geocaches in the area. At the event, provide name tags to help people start to get to know each other. Have fun, eat, and do a little geocaching. Afterward, make sure you have everyone's name, phone number, and e-mail address so that you can organize the group and plan the next event.

When you have a group of people interested, start a website or use a group forum (for instance, Yahoo! Groups). Use your new web home to post membership information, photos, resources, and details of the next event. Group message boards allow members to post information and keep in touch. Be creative with your events and the member list will continue to grow. There are a lot of fun and interesting things for a group to do: hide a group geocache, have a barbecue, camp out, invite special guests, host training seminars, visit historical or interesting outdoor places, and organize community projects. Involve members by asking them to come up with ideas and help plan the next events.

As your group grows, give it some organization. Its structure could be very informal, as long as projects are assigned to members who will follow through to keep things going. At some point, you'll need a leader, a treasurer, and someone organized enough to keep track of everything. The group can raise a little money to pay for web fees or T-shirts.

The main thing is for everyone to have fun. Don't bog the group down with meetings, politics, or business. People go geocaching to get away from those things. Use the get-togethers as opportunities to meet fellow geocachers and get outdoors more often.

Geocaching Events

From the early beginnings of geocaching, people wanted to share information, ideas, and locations; it was only natural for this online sharing to move offline. Event caches get geocachers to discuss and share their common bond, geocaching. Events are held in a wide variety of locations, from meeting halls to local parks, but are always created for and by geocachers.

Don't forget about geocaching kids when planning an event. Kid-friendly activities and goodies, like these tattoos, can be great additions to any event.
(Steve Hanes)

You can find a list of upcoming geocaching events on the front page of Geocaching.com. However, given the growth of the activity and the huge number of events that take place every month, the list on the front page is often less than what is actually taking place. Click on the link to view the full Event Calendar.

On the Event Calendar you will find state, region, and country listings of events happening on any given day. If you see one that appears to be in your area, simply click on the link for that day and follow it to the detailed event page.

Geocaching events are also promoted through the Groundspeak Weekly Notification e-mail that is available to any registered geocacher on an opt-in basis. Any event that is occurring within your local area will be listed in the weekly e-mail.

EUREKA!

Organizing an event can be a lot of fun. Events are submitted to Geocaching.com much like other geocaches. However, make sure you post the event at least two weeks prior to the date so that potential attendees have sufficient notice to make plans.

There are many different types of geocaching events and many regions develop events that take on their own style. One of the most common types of events is simply the Meet 'n' Greet. These are relaxed, informal meetings that normally take place at restaurants in reserved meeting areas. Meet 'n' Greets are great opportunities to sit down and get to know the other geocachers in the area.

Other events take on more of a competitive flavor with special games and competitions set up by the event organizers. Many of these traditional events take place in large parks where geocaches might be hidden specifically to be found at the event. Prizes are often awarded and usually there is a large picnic or potluck meal that everyone enjoys.

As with the traditional geocache type, the event cache type has also evolved over time with community contribution and now includes the original Event Cache, Mega-Event Cache, and CITO Event.

Mega-Event Cache

In 2003, a Tennessee geocacher named JoGPS had a vision. His dream was to host a geocaching event that would bring people from all over the country, and possibly all over the world. Taking a cue from his younger days, he called the event, "GeoWoodstock." Since that first event, GeoWoodstock has become an annually celebrated event and continues to grow in global attendance and excitement.

Here is a group photo of GeoWoodstock attendees who have attended the annual event every year since its inception! Bottom row: Show Me the Cache, mtn-man, koneko. Middle row: WCNUT & TATER, Turtle3863, Southpaw. Top row: robertlipe, JoGPS.

(Tina Lampton)

As GeoWoodstock saw success in attendance, other similar geocaching events began to be established around the world. In response to community excitement and innovation, Groundspeak created a unique event cache type: The Mega Event. This is a special designation reserved for event caches, where among other requirements, there are at least 500 attendees. A Mega-Event Cache may be published up to one year prior to the event date and typically attracts geocachers from all over the world.

Cache In Trash Out Events—Giving Back and Having Fun

Geocachers will use any excuse to get together, but one of their favorites is Cache In Trash Out (CITO) events. As briefly discussed in Chapter 2, CITO is an ongoing environmental initiative supported by the geocaching community. Since 2002, geocachers have been dedicated to cleaning up parks and other cache-friendly places around the world. Many geocachers carry a garbage bag and pick up trash on their way to and from a geocache. It is one of the ways in which geocachers help preserve the natural beauty of our outdoor resources.

A CITO Event is an event held for the specific purpose of getting geocachers together to clean up an area. CITO Events are often held in cooperation with local park departments or community organizations. They're a great way to emphasize geocachers' interest and support of the environment.

Although an ongoing effort, Groundspeak celebrates an Annual International CITO Event where geocachers have an opportunity to participate in coordinated worldwide clean-up efforts. Geocachers host clean-up events in their local areas on the same day or weekend as other geocachers around the world. Events can focus simply on trash removal or can take on park improvement projects. CITO events are not only a fun way to get geocachers together but also make positive social and environmental impacts in our communities.

Organizing Your Own Geocaching Event

So now that you have attended a few geocaching events, are you ready to host your own? Great! But there is much planning to do in order to ensure a successful gathering. Here is a list of topics to consider when organizing your event:

- **Communicate event goals.** What is the purpose of the event? Is this a Meet 'n' Greet at a local pub or a potluck where attendees should bring a dish to share? Perhaps you intend to gather folks for trail maintenance where gloves and resources would be beneficial? Clearly state the event expectations so that geocachers know what to anticipate. Remember, geocaching events should be free to participants.

- **Location, location, location.** The success of your event will be highly dependent on the location you choose.

  For an outdoor event, find a large park or outdoor area where you can get permission to hold the event. Reserve the location and secure whatever permit you need far in advance. Find an area that is interesting for geocaching and that includes basic amenities such as parking, shelter, and bathrooms.

  For an indoor event, try to find a location where there are no entry or rental room fees. Ask in advance about large parties and potential payment options if you anticipate a large number of attendees ordering food and beverages. Make sure to also consider the ages of potential attendees, especially children. If you choose a particular location, will children be able to attend? Clearly communicate this information in advance. Finally, in metro areas, consider available transportation and parking needs.

- **Organization is key.** Before the event, post as many details as possible. For the event, put together a program or information board explaining event details. It is always a good idea to decide in advance what to do if it rains.

- **Plan in advance.** Post Mega Events at least six months in advance. This gives participants the opportunity to take the time off to attend. Also, campgrounds and lodging may be booked long in advance. Make sure lodging and camping is available if you are planning a weekend-long event.

  To also ensure good attendance, do not forget to check the online event calendar on Geocaching.com to review potential event conflicts in the area.

- **Make sure everyone has fun!** Keep things simple and the mood light. Even if you are hoping to have some competitive games, don't let the atmosphere become so intense that it overrides the ability of people to simply enjoy themselves.

EUREKA!

Many people are adding educational opportunities to their geocaching events by providing seminars on various topics relating to navigation, GPS, and geocaching.

A variety of games helps keep an event interesting and fun. You can offer a number of game variations to keep players engaged. Here are some commonly used basics:

- **Traditional timed cache events.** Participants attempt to find as many caches as possible within a specified time limit. Each cache contains tickets or envelopes taken by the finders to verify they were there. Some form of handicap system could be used to allow older and younger teams to compete with the highly experienced or athletic ones.

- **Hide and seek.** Participants provide their own cache containers and hide them for the officials to find. Players are judged by their creativity in creating and hiding the caches. Some players have become very innovative and have made custom cache containers out of hollowed logs and pinecones.

- **Puzzle caches.** Use your imagination to come up with games to keep players guessing and using their creativity. One example is to place items in caches that, when found, require participants to make something with the contents. Another idea might be to have players find envelopes containing trivia questions. Players receive points for questions answered correctly.

With creativity and good organization skills, your event will undoubtedly be a great success.

The Least You Need to Know

- Participation in a geocaching group is a great way to keep in contact with fellow geocachers and be a positive influence in your community.

- Use the Geocaching.com and/or regional discussion forums to keep up on the latest GPS news and geocaching activity developments.

- Geocachers love to share their personal stories and experiences while geocaching. From online forum posts to podcasts and blogs, geocachers have a great number of opportunities to learn from one another.

- Geocaching events are a great way to meet new geocachers and to celebrate geocaching.

- Cache In Trash Out events bring geocachers together to beautify their parks and communities.

Geocaching While on Vacation

In This Chapter

- Working geocaching into your vacation plans
- Helping Travel Bugs find their way
- Packing for a geocaching vacation

If you are heading off on a trip, don't forget to bring along your GPS receiver! Traveling with your device is not only a good way to minimize the stress of navigating an unfamiliar area, but it is also an excellent way to explore unique locations.

While most people may be inclined to use their devices to search only for hotels, restaurants, and other points of interest, geocachers learn to take advantage of the more unknown tourist destinations—the local geocaches placed in the area!

By now you have found a few geocaches and have probably realized that people place geocaches in areas that they consider to be special. When you travel, seeking out the local geocaches is a great way to find some exceptional places and adventures that don't show up in the traditional guide books. In this chapter, we discuss how to easily go geocaching when you travel, including what items to bring, and how to identify the must-do geocaches in the area.

Planning Your Trip

Input geocaches into your receiver a few days before leaving on your trip. The best method is to create a Pocket Query on Geocaching. com and have this e-mailed to you for download into your device. Among other things, a Pocket Query allows you to filter by geocache type, distance from a known point, and cache attributes so that you can get the best list of geocaches possible for where you are traveling and what you will have time to search for. Depending on the amount of free time you'll have, you may want to consider filtering out multi-caches and mystery caches, as these normally take longer to complete. Depending on your level of geocaching expertise, you also might want to limit your Pocket Query to caches with lower terrain and difficulty ratings for the same reason.

On the other hand, if you have time to explore, take a closer look at what the area has to offer. You might find some interesting EarthCaches that will not only be fun but educational. You also might discover one or two caches that are considered must-dos in the area. Look closely at any bookmark lists you find on local geocache detail pages. Geocachers often create lists of their favorite geocaches in an area. You can glean a lot from the experiences of others.

Geocaching while on a family vacation can be memorable.
(Alan Torrigino)

If you are really looking for some of the special, not-to-miss geo-caches in your travels, be sure to search the regional forums on Geocaching.com or consider posting a request for suggestions. Traveling geocachers post notes asking for cache suggestions or links to the local geocaching groups where local geocachers can provide resources and advice. Chances are good that you can even find a geocaching buddy and tour guide for all the geocache-finding and sightseeing you can handle. If not, you will at least be equipped with local knowledge of the must-do geocaches in the area.

Geocaching Vacations

Many geocachers actually plan their vacations around well-known destinations for geocaching. For example, some geocachers pride themselves on having found a geocache in every U.S. state while others would like to find one of every unique geocache type. Whatever the motivation, this desire to travel has not escaped the notice of the travel and tourism industry. Recently, more and more geocaching packages are being offered as enticements to travelers.

Hotels and bed-and-breakfasts are beginning to offer geocaching adventure packages in addition to their more traditional wedding and spa packages. These hotels will often loan you a GPS device, provide instructions and coordinates for use, and even pack a picnic lunch for you to enjoy on your outing.

Visitor centers and tourist bureaus are also creating interpretive programs using GPS and geocaching. These programs promise tourists scenic vistas, historic settings, education, and plenty of geocaches to find along the way.

If you are looking for an adventure on water, don't dismiss a cruise. Geocaching on cruises is becoming more popular as a shore excursion. With over 700,000 geocaches hidden around the world, you can geocache while sailing to Alaska or the Caribbean and just about anywhere else.

Travelin' Bugs

Regardless of the distance you plan to travel, it is great to bring along a Travel Bug or two—especially if you are going to an area with a major or international airport. If the bug has a goal to travel a great distance, you can easily drop it off at a *Travel Bug Hotel.* These are popular geocache sites that are often found next to major airports, making Travel Bugs easy to find and take overseas.

GEO-LINGO

Travel Bug Hotels are geocaches set up primarily for the purpose of holding Travel Bugs for transfer. Feel free to drop a Travel Bug off or pick one up when you visit these locations.

Some Travel Bugs ask that you take them along on vacation. A geocacher named "Mandrew" wanted to take his dad on vacation for Father's Day in 2005 but couldn't, so he sent a Travel Bug instead. "Dad's Vacation" has traveled over 4,000 miles and visited the NASA Space Center in Huntsville, Alabama, and the west coast of Florida. Not a bad trip for a Travel Bug from Wisconsin!

By paying attention to a Travel Bug's goal you can be sure to take it to some views that the owner is sure to appreciate.
(Olaf Pfeiffer)

Not to be outdone, a Travel Bug named, "Mom on vacation!!" traveled over 52,000 miles and saw everything from California to New Jersey before heading across the ocean and ending up in Tasmania!

Meaningful Places

Much of the enjoyment of travel is to visit places of special meaning, like historical sites, awesome vistas, or places that represent our families' roots. These places inspire us and help us appreciate our ancestors who contributed so much to what our lives are today. Through geocaching, travelers have a reason to see and experience these locations they would probably never see otherwise.

If the site is local, hiding a geocache is a way to allow travelers to appreciate a unique area in your community. Place information in the cache explaining why you chose this location, why it's special, and what visitors should look for to appreciate its history.

When traveling, it is tempting to place a geocache in a location that you found exceptionally beautiful or that has special meaning to you. However, please realize that placing geocaches outside your home area is discouraged. Caches need to be maintained and that is difficult to do if you live far away. If the geocache gets wet or damaged you need to be able to easily repair or replace it in a timely manner. If you are unable to do so, you shouldn't place a geocache in the area. Generally, vacation caches will not be published on Geocaching.com due to the ongoing maintenance requirement.

Packing for Vacation Geocaching

Self-described nerd Markus explains a dilemma that many of us have. "Let's see, swimsuit, sunblock, sunglasses, ... When you're a technology-obsessed nerd, it's not quite so simple." Markus assembled all the electronic gear needed for a geocaching trip across the desert southwest of the United States. Obviously, most of us do not require this many electronics, but it's a fun example of techno-travel accessorizing. Besides, even this much gear is still lighter than a bag of golf clubs!

Imagine how much fun it is to try to get this stuff through airport security!
(Markus Wandal)

Approximately top left to bottom right, we have:

- Laptop computer for storing digital pictures, GPS data, and GPS mapping software
- Power supply and line cord for the laptop
- Power inverter, to use line-powered gadgets in the car
- Cigarette-lighter plug expander
- Compact flash adapter, for reading digital camera memory cards
- GPS receiver case (a cell phone case)
- Digital camera and case
- Spare digital camera batteries
- Charger for digital camera batteries
- Spare batteries for headlamp
- LED headlamp
- Spare batteries for GPS receiver

- GPS receiver
- Cigarette-lighter extension cord
- AC extension cord (for use with power inverter)
- AC multiplug
- Charging base for FRS (two-way) radios
- Belt clips for FRS radios
- FRS radios
- Auto power/data cable for GPS

Ah, the modern convenience of it all.

International Considerations

When traveling internationally to geocache, it makes sense to pack some additional resources to help you find your way around and adjust to the local customs and requirements. Some of these items may include guidebooks, language translators, international power adapters, and international maps (both electronic and traditional printed maps).

You may also want to post a topic to the International section of the Geocaching.com discussion forums for the country to which you are traveling. You can ask locals for cool cache recommendations or even tips on local travel, restaurants, and other accommodations.

Flying with GPS

As great as the temptation might seem, don't turn your receiver on while flying on a commercial plane without first asking the flight attendants. Although seeing where you are as you fly over a country may sound like fun, this sort of thing is often frowned upon by airline crews. Their common response is that receivers and other electronic devices could interfere with the plane's own navigation system. In these days of heightened security there is no reason to cause concern or draw unnecessary attention to yourself.

If flying with GPS receivers, computers, and cameras, it is often best to pack them in a sturdy case and carry them onto the plane. This helps prevent the gear from becoming lost or stolen.

Use Some GPS Discretion

Before turning on your receiver, be aware of your surroundings. It is wise not to use a GPS receiver around any areas where you might be perceived to be suspicious. For example, you may wish to avoid using your GPS or other electronics in close proximity to embassies, military bases, and other prominent government buildings. Obviously, some parts of the world are more sensitive to this than others. The last thing you want to do is extend your trip with lengthy interrogations by authorities. Be forewarned: It is not uncommon for "officials" to determine that your gear is better than theirs, so that they will let you off with a warning and relieve you of that unnecessary travel baggage.

> **DEAD BATTERIES**
>
> Use a GPS receiver in the wrong place at the wrong time and you could be considered a spy. In 1997, a Qualcomm wireless communication engineer was charged with espionage by Russian authorities. Richard L. Bliss was using a GPS receiver while installing a cellular phone system in the city of Rostov-on-Don. The Russian agents that arrested him insisted he was spying on secret sites.

The Least You Need to Know

- Geocaching is a great way to explore unique locations while traveling.
- The travel and tourism industry is beginning to use geocaching as an activity to encourage visitation.
- Bringing Travel Bugs along can liven up your next vacation.
- Use caution when using your GPS device while traveling abroad to avoid security problems. Do not use it around sensitive areas such as embassies and government buildings.

The Future of GPS Games

If you thought geocaching was fun, hold onto something, because GPS gaming continues to evolve!

Developments in GPS-enabled devices make it easier than ever to find geocaches, but geocaching is just the beginning in a new world of location-based mobile entertainment. Ready to learn more?

In Part 5, you are introduced to new concepts in location-based gaming, including two projects from Groundspeak called Waymarking and Wherigo.

Waymarking— It's Virtually a Whole New Game

In The Chapter

- Find out what waymarking is
- Log your first visit to a waymark
- Create your own waymarks
- Create your own waymarking category

Walk into your local library and you're immediately confronted with shelf after shelf of books. Depending on the size of the library it could take hours or days to find what you are looking for. However, thanks to a catalog or online system you can search for the book you want by title, subject, author, and a variety of other criteria and have the book in your hand in mere minutes.

What if the locations of the world could be cataloged like that? Imagine being able to search for buildings, land formations, monuments, and thousands of other objects around the world by category and then locate them with GPS accuracy. That's the idea behind waymarking, a user-generated collection of unique and interesting locations around the world.

In this chapter, you'll learn about the early beginnings of waymarking, how to participate, and finally, how to contribute to this growing worldwide community.

What Is Waymarking?

Developed by Groundspeak, waymarking is a way to mark unique locations on the planet, provide related information for those locations, and categorize them for easy reference and sharing. While GPS technology enables users to pinpoint any location on the planet, mark the location, and share it with others, waymarking is the toolset for categorizing and adding unique information for that location.

The waymarking website at Waymarking.com contains over 800 unique location categories, such as fishing holes, historical markers, covered bridges, and abstract public sculptures. Each category is managed by a group of waymarking participants, casually called *waymarkers*, who define the category and then review and approve all qualified waymark submissions for that category.

 GEO-LINGO

A **waymarker** is a casual term used to describe a waymarking enthusiast, someone that actively participates in the waymarking community.

A New Game with Deep Roots

In the early days of geocaching, as the game was still developing, the creativity of the players led to the development of new geocache types. Multi-caches, mystery caches, and even events were all born out of a desire to do something different than the standard "box hidden in the woods."

One of the early geocache variations was virtual caches. Unlike a physical cache, virtual caches had no containers. Instead, the location itself was what the virtual cache owner wanted to share with you. Oftentimes, virtual geocaches took people to unique spots or monuments and required answering a question or posting a picture as proof of the visit since there was no physical logbook to sign.

Over time, the qualifications for what made a good virtual cache began to blur. Geocacher opinions varied on what they believed to be a worthy experience. Many also wondered why a virtual cache would be placed if the actual physical location could have just as easily supported a cache container instead.

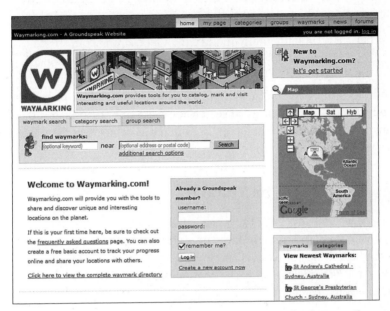

The Waymarking.com homepage, where almost any spot on the planet can be cataloged and searched for.
(Waymarking.com)

At the same time, another type of geocache known as a *locationless cache* was beginning to present its own set of difficulties. Locationless caches, or *reverse geocaches* were a type of geocache where the job of the geocacher was to find a location that matched the category set up by the owner. For example, if the cache owner's category was *"Natural Land Bridges,"* the geocacher would have to find a place that matched that category and record the coordinates for that location (often accompanied by a picture).

While the idea of locationless caches was enjoyed by many playing the game, the results were difficult to manage. Geocaching.com had not been created to support the type of content that was being logged. For instance, a single locationless cache page would contain thousands of "finds" from all over the world. In order to access a specific find, one would have to scroll through thousands of logs on the geocache details page in order to find the unique location content. While it was clear that people loved creating unique content as part of the game, the results taxed the Geocaching.com site and made it difficult to truly mark and then later reference those locations.

Rather than fundamentally modify the Geocaching.com site to address virtual and locationless caches, Groundspeak developed a new, dedicated site. Waymarking.com was designed to handle virtual and locationless caches more appropriately, by providing people the opportunity to organize and search for these unique locations by category. This change organized places in a way that made them both searchable and fun to find.

Person, Place, or Thing?

In geocaching there are those who enjoy seeking caches and others who enjoy hiding. Similarly, in waymarking there are those who enjoy searching for objects and locations that match a specific category and others who enjoy the challenge of creating and managing a waymarking category.

The waymark category directory works in a hierarchical format, moving from general categories to specific categories and then to the individual waymarks. One top-level category might begin with "Art/Music," then contain a subcategory of "Statues," and be followed by yet another subcategory of "Insect Sculptures." From here you will find individual waymarks that have been located and cataloged by individual players. The waymark might be a 10-foot tall praying mantis in North Carolina or the Boll Weevil Monument in Enterprise, Alabama. The key is that each individual waymark fits within the specified parameters of the categories containing the waymark.

Getting Started with Waymarking

With hundreds of categories and over 150,000 waymark listings worldwide, getting started with waymarking is easy.

Searching for a Waymark

On the Waymarking.com site, you can search for waymarks using postal code, keyword, coordinates, or address. Once your search is complete, you can view all of the search results to find a location or object that interests you. You can view waymark details, see photos, and read logs from others who have visited that waymark.

Once you've found one that you'd like to visit, you can enter the coordinates into your GPS receiver to take you there, just like finding a geocache! Location coordinates are prominently displayed on each waymark detail page and can be entered either by hand or downloaded in a file format for use in a number of applications.

As with geocaching, be sure to read the waymark detail page before heading outdoors. There you will find information about the location you are visiting as well as instructions on how to log your visit to the waymark. Oftentimes the waymark owner will request a picture or some other information as valid proof that you actually visited the site.

After you've visited a particular waymark location and met the waymark requirements, you can return to the waymark detail page on Waymarking.com and log your visit online. Waymark visits are recorded much like geocache visits, complete with the ability to add your comments and photographs.

Even if you don't plan to physically visit a particular location, the waymarking site can provide hours of entertainment. Have fun exploring interesting and unique places, almost like a virtual tourist, from around the world!

Creating Your Own Waymark

The number of waymark categories continues to grow. Much of the growth is due to the wide variety of topics that people are interested in and feel passionate about. With over 800 categories currently listed, there is something for everyone to appreciate and enjoy.

As with individual waymarks, you can also search for waymarking categories using keywords. For example, if you are interested in firehouses, entering "firehouses" into the keyword search turns up two categories. "Converted Firehouses" is for buildings that formerly were used as firehouses but now might be used as restaurants, museums, or even private residences. "Firehouses" itself is a category for buildings currently used for the storage of fire-fighting apparatus and related equipment.

Perhaps you would like to add your local firehouse to the waymark category. Clicking on the category name brings up a short description of what the category group is looking for. From here, you can click for more detailed information on how to create your own waymark for the category.

Waymark categories are managed by individual groups responsible for all the activity within the designated category. The group creates the category description and assigns the parameters for allowing waymarks to be listed in the category. The group then manages the category information by deciding which waymarks do and do not fit within the category as specified by them.

After you have obtained coordinates for the location, as well as all required information for waymark listings in that category, you can submit your own waymark listing. Click the "Post New Waymark" link on the right side of the category page and complete the required information. If pictures are required, click the "Upload Images" link at the top of the page. When you're ready, click the "Preview and Submit" button to make any further changes or submit the page for review.

Your waymark will be reviewed by the category management group after you submit it. If it fits the established parameters for the category, it will be approved. If it doesn't fit the parameters, or if required information is missing, it may be declined or you might be asked to make changes or provide more information.

Your waymark will be available for others to visit and enjoy once it is approved and published on the site. You will be notified whenever your waymark listing is logged, and you will have the satisfaction of knowing that someone visited your waymark and that you contributed to an ever-growing list of locations around the world.

A sample waymark page in the "Firehouses" category.
(Bruce Seeling)

Creating Your Own Waymarking Category

After spending some time getting involved with waymarking, you may find that there are unique locations or objects that just don't seem to fit well in the current list of categories. Maybe there's a topic that has always interested you or some land formation that you would like to feature. If the topic doesn't exist yet, you can get more involved and create your own category to manage.

> **EUREKA!**
>
> Some waymarking categories have the potential to be useful for people doing research. Because waymarks are often found by people who are simply searching for information online, waymark owners have been known to be contacted by people seeking permission to use their information and photos!

Criteria for Becoming a Category Manager

In order to create your own category, you need to be a Premium Member of Groundspeak. This requirement was set by Groundspeak in order to ensure that each category manager has a vested interest in the category and associated waymarks she manages. Remember, waymarking, like geocaching, is an activity that is built around community. If a community member does not care about the information she approves, it is unlikely that the location or information related to it will be enjoyed, trusted, or respected.

Groundspeak also learned early on that having a single person manage a category could cause some frustrating delays in getting new waymarks reviewed. Most people don't have the time to refresh the website every few minutes, waiting for new waymark submissions to review. What would happen if someone fell ill or went on vacation? To address these issues, Groundspeak developed the concept of group category management as a way for multiple people who care about a category to share the workload in its review. As a result, at least three Premium Members are now required in order to create and manage a category.

Creating a new waymark category requires you to enter the category name, description, and any requirements for waymarks submitted to the category.
(Bret Hammond)

Getting Your Category Approved

So are you ready to create your own category? A great place to find others who are interested in managing a waymark category is in the Waymarking.com discussion forums. Once you have your group assembled, you can fill out the category submission page. Because people search for category names, you should name your category in a way that clearly describes the waymarks contained within it. Try to avoid puns and plays on words. If your category represents lighthouses, you wouldn't want to call it "Light My Way." The better choice would be simply "Lighthouses." Individual waymarks, not categories, are better suited for creative titles.

One of the great things about creating a waymark category is that you are also able to define the information that will be required for each waymark. So, for a "Coffee Shop" category, you may want to know each waymark's hours of operation, phone number, brand of coffee served, and whether it has free Wi-Fi access. For a "Covered Bridges" category, you may want to know the length of the bridge, year of construction, and construction material. So, carefully consider the type of waymarks you are interested in, and make sure to include fields for valuable and relevant information.

Submit your category for "Peer Review" after you complete the waymark category page. Peer Review consists of a queue available to all Premium Members, allowing them to review, vote, and comment on category hopefuls. Voting lasts for three days and is completely anonymous. As a general rule of thumb, a two-thirds majority is necessary to approve a category for inclusion in the category list. In the case where a category decision is on the fence, Groundspeak reserves the right to make the final decision. In most close cases, however, Groundspeak will approve the category. One of the things to keep in mind when voting on categories is that some people have a different idea of what is worthy of inclusion in the category list. If you think a number of people will enjoy the category, even if it doesn't particularly interest you personally, you should vote "yea" and perhaps give some recommendations for improvement.

Occasionally a category will not pass Peer Review. If that happens, the category will be archived and your group will need to start over.

It's not recommended to submit the same category to Peer Review more than a couple times.

If your category is approved, you have the important job of being a category manager. As a category manager it is your responsibility to determine the rules, with help from your group officers, for posting of waymarks to your new category.

The Grid

Do you remember reading about geocachers and how some liked to have found at least one of each of the unique geocache types? Imagine that same idea for waymarking, but rather than just a few unique types, there are hundreds! To keep track of all of the categories, a grid was introduced on participant profile pages on Waymarking.com. The grid is a visual representation of all of the waymarks that an individual has visited and submitted to the site. Because each category is represented by a unique pixel art icon, many users strive to submit or visit waymarks from all different categories so that they can fill up their grid with all of the unique icons. A full, or mostly full, grid has become a badge of honor among avid waymarking participants.

EUREKA!

The distinctive, art-style icons and city-scapes found on Waymarking.com represent *pixel art*. Many waymarkers enjoy the pixel art representations of each waymarking category.

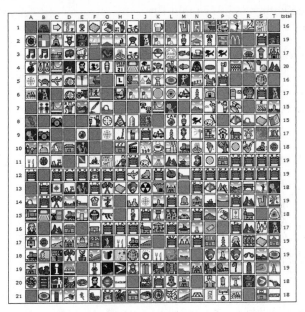

The Grid of BruceS from Waymarking.com.
(Bruce Seeling)

The Least You Need to Know

- Waymarking is a GPS activity where participants mark unique locations on the planet and then share the locations online.

- In its simplest form, waymarking can be considered a scavenger hunt for unique and interesting locations in the world.

- A waymark category holds all the waymarks specific to that category's theme. Each waymark category has specific submission requirements that are created and evaluated by its category managers.

- Waymark categories are managed by individual groups responsible for all the activity within its assigned category.

- Being a part of a group is a great way to contribute to the growing waymarking community. Help mark the world!

Wherigo—The Next Generation of GPS-Enabled Adventures

16

In This Chapter

- Discover what Wherigo is
- Learn how to play
- Understand the Wherigo geocache type
- Find out how to build your own Wherigo experience

What if you could bring your favorite adventure video game into the outdoor world using GPS technology? Can you imagine an experience where participants have to physically move around in the real world to accomplish tasks, interact with characters, and complete goals? Back in 2001, when Geocaching.com was first created, the founders of Groundspeak began to research and develop ideas that would do just that. Passionate about location, they created what was to be called Wherigo, a platform for creating location-based games in the real world.

In this chapter we discuss Wherigo, its early beginnings and evolution, its tie-in to the geocaching community, and its potential use in location-based entertainment.

What Is Wherigo?

If you are familiar with adventure games like Zork, Myst, or the Secret of Monkey Island, you can think of Wherigo as an adventure game construction set for the real world. Unlike these traditional video games, however, with Wherigo you don't type "north" or click your mouse to move your character around on a computer screen. Instead, participants literally move themselves in the real world and interact with objects and characters using a handheld GPS-enabled device.

The Wherigo.com homepage where you can search for cartridges and download the Wherigo Builder and Player Applications.
(Wherigo.com)

If you are thinking that this sounds a little complicated, do not worry. We will discuss the details of how Wherigo works later in the chapter. But first things first: you must evaluate your resources. Just as in geocaching and waymarking where people can participate in a number of ways, Wherigo allows people to be both builders and players of these unique, outdoor experiences.

The Wherigo platform includes a Wherigo Player Application and a Wherigo Builder Application, both available for free online at Wherigo.com. To play, one must search for and download an experience, called a *cartridge*, and load this into a compatible GPS device.

GEO-LINGO

Cartridge is a term used to describe the experience created by a Wherigo Builder. It is not a physical object but a self-contained file that is downloaded from Wherigo.com and then run using the Wherigo Player Application and a compatible GPS device.

Get in Gear—Equipment for Playing

If you're interested in playing a Wherigo experience outdoors, you have to look to a whole new generation of GPS devices. Due to the advanced feature set of Wherigo, these devices have more in common with your computer than with your compass. Currently, you can participate in Wherigo using most GPS-enabled Pocket PC devices, as well as Garmin's Colorado and Oregon handheld GPS units. Groundspeak is also currently working to bring the Wherigo platform to other GPS-enabled devices, including mobile phones.

If you're a Pocket PC user, you may already have the equipment needed. Many PDA's have built-in GPS receivers, while many others can connect either by wire or wirelessly to GPS receivers.

Here is a partial list of handheld devices that work with the Wherigo Player Application:

- AT&T 8525
- Dell Axim X3
- Dell Axim X51v
- Garmin Colorado
- Garmin iQue M4
- Garmin iQue M5
- Garmin Oregon
- Many models of HP iPAQ
- HTC Touch Cruise

- Mio A201

- Mio P350 PDA

- Mitac Mio 168

- Palm Treo 700WX phone

- Verizon XV6700

The Garmin Colorado was the first dedicated recreational GPS device to include Wherigo as a preloaded application.
(Image used courtesy © of Garmin Ltd. or its affiliates. Copyright Garmin Ltd. or its affiliates.)

If you are using either a Garmin Colorado or Oregon GPS, you likely have the Wherigo Player Application preloaded onto your device. However, it is always wise to check Wherigo.com to ensure that you have the latest Wherigo Player installed. If you intend to play with a Pocket PC, you need to download the free Wherigo Player Application from Wherigo.com and install it on your device.

Once the Wherigo Player is installed on your Pocket PC, you're ready to download a game cartridge and get out and play!

If you do not have access to a compatible GPS device, you can still experience Wherigo! Download the free Wherigo Builder Application and use the builder to "emulate" a cartridge. While not the intended use, the emulator allows you to drag a character from location to location online, simulating what you would have experienced real-time outdoors. Many Wherigo builders use this as a tool of inspiration and innovation, reviewing unique cartridges from around the world so that they can build experiences of their own!

Wherigo: Getting into the Game

Now that you have downloaded a cartridge and loaded it into your GPS-enabled device, you are ready to head outdoors. But wait, let's discuss what you can expect.

Redefining Location

Wherigo cartridges are created by people who want to share a unique experience with you. A cartridge will likely direct you to a number of locations, similar to a multistage geocache, asking you to speak to characters or complete tasks along the way. However, unlike with geocaching or waymarking, where you navigate to a specific point using coordinates, in Wherigo, you navigate to a shape in the world.

The basic building block of a Wherigo experience is called a *zone*. A zone is essentially a predefined shape. For instance, if you were to draw a shape on a paper map, say outlining a city block, this defined area would be called a zone. Zones can be big or small, and round, square, or any other shape as defined by an author. In other words, a zone is a predefined area marked by several waypoints.

As you walk into this zone or shape in the real world, events and actions can occur. So, for example, a Wherigo author can show a player a set of instructions to proceed to a certain location. As the player gets within 100 feet of the location, the author can show the player a message that says, "You are getting close!" When the player gets closer and enters the predefined zone, the author can show the player an image of a character and play an audio file that says, "Congratulations, you made it! I am glad you're here."

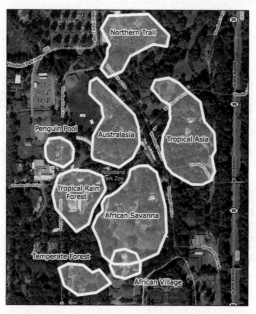

A map of the zones shown in the "Penguin Escape" Cartridge. This cartridge takes players on a fun and interactive adventure through Seattle's Woodland Park Zoo.
(Groundspeak)

How does Wherigo work? When your GPS device detects that you have entered a zone, the Wherigo software responds with an event that the author has programmed into the game. As a player moves in and out of different zones within a Wherigo cartridge, he might encounter a virtual character on his screen who will give him information he needs to continue the game. Or, he might be given a virtual object (such as a key) to place in his inventory to use later in the game.

EUREKA!

Several different types of media can be incorporated in a Wherigo cartridge. Some include sound effects when entering different zones or completing certain tasks. However, note that not all devices are designed to play sound files.

Understanding How to Play

Now that you understand how to navigate to a zone or location, let's learn about the other components of play.

Within the Wherigo playing experience, there are potentially four main areas of focus: "Locations," "You See," "Inventory," and "Tasks."

- **Locations.** The zones within a cartridge. A location can contain characters and items (both real and imaginary) that a player can interact with. Players mostly interact with locations by entering and exiting the predefined areas.

- **You See.** A list of items (can be characters or objects) that the player's character can see from the current location of the character. You can often click on items you see to investigate them further.

- **Inventory.** A collection of items that belong to a player. It is helpful to think of it as a virtual backpack for storing items obtained during the game. For instance, if an author created a murder mystery cartridge, she might make you collect virtual clues that will enable you to catch the killer as part of the experience. If it's a science fiction adventure, you might collect alien artifacts or fuel cells to refuel your rocket.

- **Tasks.** Typically used by an author to help direct the playing experience. This is simply a list of all tasks that need to be completed in the cartridge. Some tasks do not show up on the list until you receive them in the game or accomplish other tasks. Since Wherigo cartridges can be linear or nonlinear, it helps to check the "Tasks" every now and then just to make sure you are on the right path to completing the cartridge.

As the Wherigo adventure progresses, you might find yourself needing to complete certain tasks set up by the author of the game. You may need to unlock a virtual door with a virtual key that you picked up earlier. If the game is taking you on a tour of a city, you might be asked to walk to a certain landmark and enter another zone to continue the game. In an adventure cartridge, the task might require you to complete mini-quests before continuing the main adventure.

To add to the challenge, the game author may also include a question to be answered of the player (called an *input*) or integrate the use of a timer for completing tasks. So, for example, you may have to reach a particular destination within a certain timeframe. The rest of the adventure can depend on whether you make it or not.

 GEO-LINGO

An **input** is a way for a Wherigo author to ask a player a question. The question is displayed in a window on the device, where the user can then respond to it. There are three types of inputs: Text (where the player uses an onscreen keyboard to type in an answer), Multiple Choice (the player chooses one of several options via a list of buttons), and True/False.

More than Just a Game

Wherigo is unique in that it is a platform that can be used to create diverse experiences. The Wherigo Builder and tools available are designed to be open-ended, so Wherigo cartridge builders can create any number of interesting experiences for a player. Here are some examples of what can be created with the Wherigo Builder:

- A walking tour of city sights
- A neighborhood scavenger hunt
- An interactive fictional adventure
- A tour of historic sites or landmarks
- An alternate reality game

In addition to games that are location specific, it's also possible to play games designed to be played anywhere. These are called "Play Anywhere Cartridges." The zones for these cartridges are not predefined; they are generated based on where the player is when he starts the cartridge. Although they are a bit more complicated to create, these cartridges can be played by many more people all over the world. To play these cartridges, all that is normally needed is a wide-open space.

One example of a Play Anywhere cartridge is the Wherigo Player Tutorial. This Tutorial comes preloaded on the Garmin Colorado and Oregon series of GPS units and can also be downloaded for free at Wherigo.com. It is a 15-minute space adventure game that teaches the basics of the Wherigo game and player interface. It gives you a good idea of how to play and how to move around within a Wherigo cartridge.

Wherigo Geocaches

While the Wherigo game grew out of the evolution of geocaching, it hasn't completely left that world. Wherigo geocaches are a unique geocache type that incorporates the fun and fantasy of a Wherigo cartridge with an actual physical geocache container at the end.

As with the Wherigo game, geocachers seeking a Wherigo geocache must download the cartridge and complete the tasks the author has laid out. Once completed, the geocacher can log her find/adventure on both Geocaching.com and Wherigo.com.

With Wherigo caches, the possibilities are endless. Authors can create full multimedia adventures for users to experience on the way to finding a cache. For example, an author can create a virtual travel companion or character that accompanies geocachers, providing hints, puzzles, and clues along the way.

Building Your Own Wherigo Adventure

Part of the fun of geocaching is being able to share places that are special to you by hiding your own geocache. It's a personal community contribution that takes a lot of work but also has a lot of reward. Likewise, creating a Wherigo cartridge can be just as rewarding. In order to create a Wherigo experience, you need to become familiar with the aspects of the game and understand how to use the Wherigo Builder Application.

A tutorial is available on the Wherigo.com website that leads you through the basics of cartridge development. By following these tutorials you will learn how to adapt these lessons into cartridges of your own. Another great place to begin learning is on the online forums found under the "Discuss" link at the top of the Wherigo. com website. Here you can learn strategies and techniques on cartridge building from other experienced players as well as the game developers.

Once you have completed and tested your cartridge, upload it online at Wherigo.com. Players can log and rate Wherigo cartridges so that you can receive immediate feedback and reward for all of your hard work!

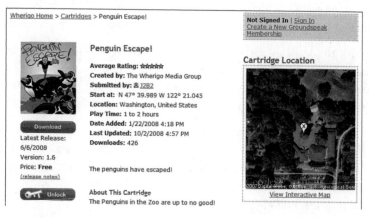

Cartridge details page for the "Penguin Escape" online at Wherigo.com.
(Wherigo.com)

The Least You Need to Know

- Wherigo is a toolset for creating and playing multimedia, location-based experiences in the real world using GPS-enabled devices.

- Wherigo requires more than just a simple GPS receiver. You must play with a device equipped to handle the software needed for the game.

- Wherigo experiences can include a limitless amount of adventures, tours, and games requiring you to interact with virtual characters, objects, and locations in the real world.

- Wherigo geocaches incorporate elements of a Wherigo experience into the search for a geocache. It's a mystery/puzzle cache with the addition of multimedia storytelling.

- There are many resources available through Wherigo.com to help people learn to build and play Wherigo cartridges.

The Future of Geocaching and GPS

In This Chapter

- Changing technology and geocaching
- Education and environmental stewardship
- Some final thoughts for ongoing success

Geocaching as an activity has long since evolved beyond the concept of finding a box in the woods. Today, geocaching is a global community of outdoor enthusiasts who create and share location-based adventures with each other.

As GPS technology has continued to develop and become more feature rich, we too, have seen the changes and innovation within geocaching. But what will happen next?

In this final chapter, we look at technology today as well as the areas of continued development in geocaching. We also consider the future of geocaching and leave you with thoughts for its continued success and sustainability as an activity.

Geocaching and Technology

Geocachers use a multi-billion dollar satellite system as a recreational tool for hours of fun and entertainment! From May 2000 until today, geocaching has grown from a single geocache hidden in rural Oregon to hundreds of thousands of geocaches being discovered in nearly every corner of the world. As GPS technology continues to evolve, there will be an increased opportunity for access. It is estimated that by 2010, 25 million people in North America will be actively using GPS. With that kind of growth in GPS use, location will undoubtedly become an integral part of people's lives.

Today, GPS and other location services are being integrated into mobile handheld devices, including cell phones, handheld gaming consoles, and dedicated recreational units. With the rise in popularity of social networking sites, people can also share messages in real time based on where they are and what they are doing. The next era of geocaching will begin to integrate these technologies as geocachers themselves innovate the way we play and communicate with one another.

EUREKA!

Geocaching applications are currently being developed for a number of cell phones, including the iPhone. Using cell phone data services and these applications, geocachers can now obtain real-time geocache data, including recently submitted cache logs, while out on the trail.

Soon, many geocachers will be geocaching with their mobile phones, sharing logs and photos with their families and friends in real time. Coordination of information related to who we are, where we are located, and what we are doing will be explored as more location-based technologies continue to be introduced.

We will also increasingly participate in activities for which GPS has been incorporated as a complementary activity. From bicycling to skiing, to horseback riding and car racing, GPS and geocaching are being used in a way that is entertaining and educational. This integration is limitless as more and more people infuse creativity in their use of GPS technology.

GPS in Education

GPS and geocaching are naturally integrated into many educational subjects, including mathematics, sciences, geography, English, social studies, history, art, health, and even physical education. Around the world, educators of all ages and experiences are integrating interactive, multimedia educational experiences around these technologies.

In the classroom, teachers utilize the experiential nature of a GPS device to get kids outdoors exploring their world. Students not only learn the curriculum in a way that can be easily remembered, they also learn important skills such as problem solving, and how to effectively communicate and collaborate as teams.

Classrooms are also supplying students with Travel Bug tags to attach to items to release into the world. In doing so, students learn about the richness of the world around them. With the ability to have stories and photos uploaded to a Travel Bug page, students learn that they can make an impact in the world, sharing and learning from people from all walks of life. Placing a geocache as a class project is also a great way to teach environmental education and stewardship as well as community ownership and responsibility.

Outside the classroom, organizations and civic groups are using GPS and geocaching as tools to not only teach but to also cultivate lasting community relationships. Schools and other civic groups, including the Boy Scouts, Girls Scouts, 4H, and more, integrate GPS usage into community projects that impact a great number of people.

A recent example of such collaborative educational programming is Bellevue, Washington's 2008 Sculptural Travel Bug Project. Teens from Bellevue's Boys and Girls Club and students from four Bellevue high schools created more than 200 small-scale sculptures out of recycled and renewable materials. Each sculpture was attached to a Travel Bug tag and released into the geocaching world. The sculptures had the goal of traveling and returning to City Hall while sharing art with the public along the way! You can find more information regarding this program at www.sculpturaltravelbugs.com/.

As another example of geocaching in education, in 2006, Groundspeak partnered with Minotaur Mazes to create the GPS Adventures Maze, an educational traveling exhibit that introduces GPS technology—its history, current uses, and future possibilities.

*Participants move through the GPS Adventures Maze and encounter a
variety of environmental differences as well as obstacles on their search
for geocaches, just like in real life!*
(Groundspeak)

Through the interactive displays and informative maze wall panels,
participants are led through a variety of environments to simulate
the experience of searching for a geocache, while learning about
diverse subjects, including the basics of traditional and current navigation, outdoor ethics, and how to prepare for heading outdoors. In
the short time the exhibit has been available, it has become a much
sought after educational resource for museums and science centers.
From children to adults, visitors love the colorful displays and interactive educational activities. As a geocacher, you will be amazed at
how well the GPS Adventures Maze captures the experience and
spirit of geocaching in the great outdoors.

EUREKA!

The GPS Adventures Maze is also a unique geocache type on Geocaching.
com. After a geocacher has visited the exhibit, he or she can log a "find"
and share his or her experience with other geocachers.

The GPS Adventures Maze is always on the move. Visit www. gpsmaze.com to find out when it will be in your area. While the use of geocaching and GPS technology in education is in its infancy, the positive impacts are already being experienced.

Environmental Ethics and Stewardship

The issue of environmental ethics and access is critical for the ongoing development and survival of geocaching as an activity. Geocaching, as well as other outdoor activities, requires access to park, rural, and wilderness lands. Yet, there can be challenges inherent in sharing these lands. Those of us who enjoy venturing into the outdoors for almost any recreational activity are occasionally confronted with individuals and organizations that would prefer all wilderness lands be closed to public access.

Another challenge faced by outdoor enthusiasts lies in dealing with the small percentage of individuals who care nothing about the outdoors. Unfortunately, this small number of people who lack consideration for the environment sometimes use lands as dumping grounds for garbage or other criminal activities. Although unrelated to geocaching, the actions of these people can sometimes lead to private and public land managers limiting land access to all, including responsible and respectful outdoor enthusiasts.

As a community, geocachers must practice good environmental stewardship and educate those who do not. If we continue to treat the environment with respect, outdoor and wilderness areas will likely be preserved and accessible for generations to come.

Like other outdoor activities, geocaching should be conducted with minimal or no impact to the environment. Generally speaking, as a group, geocachers are environmentally conscious and responsible. Geocachers are a global community composed primarily of individuals with a strong appreciation of nature. Through a demonstrated appreciation of nature and a lot of education, geocachers have worked with landowners and managers to open parks and other lands to geocaching around the world.

As geocaching continues to develop, we must continue working to overcome any negative preconceptions. Many people are unfamiliar with geocaching, and some have preconceived notions about what it is and is not. Some might have the image of geocachers digging holes and stashing junk. We need to work at educating the public, whether we are out on a trail as individuals or taking part in community projects within our geocaching organization. It's important to communicate that geocachers do not dig holes, leave garbage, or bushwhack. Our strength has always been our ability to take responsibility and hold ourselves and other geocachers accountable for all related actions as contributors to the global geocaching community.

To maintain its positive image, the geocaching community must regulate itself and remember that actions speak louder than words. Many people will judge the geocaching community, positively or negatively, based on what they actually see happening outdoors. Their perception will be based on how we conduct ourselves on the trail. Are we courteous or suspicious? Do we leave garbage behind, or help take out a little extra (*Cache In Trash Out*)? This is why working within groups and organizations can be so important.

GEO-LINGO

Cache In Trash Out (CITO) is an ongoing environmental initiative supported by the worldwide geocaching community. Since 2002, geocachers have been dedicated to cleaning up parks and other cache-friendly places around the world.

Through positive volunteer efforts, we can be effective in cultivating relationships with land agencies while helping to preserve the outdoors. Groups can also help with community and outdoor projects, for instance, by taking youth groups to a park to teach them about GPS and geocaching or by repairing a hiking trail at a favorite park.

Geocaching is about having fun in the outdoors.
(Monika Kothnig)

Where Do We Go from Here?

Thank you for taking the time to learn about geocaching and GPS technology. We are excited about the opportunity to offer this book, and appreciate having you along to learn and enjoy it. Regardless of what happens in geocaching, we hope to leave you with three final thoughts:

- Geocaching has grown rapidly and maintained a positive reputation because geocachers care about the activity and its impact in the world. Geocachers have a high level of personal ownership and accountability and go out of their way to make sure that the people are well informed about the activity and the community. This kind of positive impact will remain only as long as we continue to self-regulate the activity and each other. That means picking up after ourselves and, unfortunately, sometimes others, as well as leaving everyone we meet with a positive impression of the game and those who play it. It is an awesome responsibility, but you can rest assured that geocachers are up to the task.

- Geocaching is about having fun in the outdoors. With all the high-tech twists and turns that game variations may take, remember the basics. Although it may be just a hidden container, each geocache presents the potential for new discovery and adventure. Don't forget the simple joy of playing in the outdoors. Getting out on the trail is truly good therapy and one of life's simple pleasures, especially when shared with family and friends.

- Remember that like life, the enjoyment of the activity often lies in the journey as much as the destination. Geocaching can allow us to reflect about what is really important, while bringing us to see beautiful places, with the potential for meeting new people. Contribute to the geocaching community by sharing your journey, stories, and experiences along the way—we will all be richer for it.

Happy geocaching! We hope to meet you sometime, somewhere on the trail.

The Least You Need to Know

- Geocaching has evolved along with improvements and developments in GPS technology. It is a fun activity with a promising future.
- The success of geocaching will have much to do with the community's environmental stewardship, and our commitment to education.
- Geocaching is a way in which we can celebrate the outdoors.
- Positive sharing of your adventures contributes to the community and is key to the long-term success of geocaching.

Resource Directory

This appendix contains a list of contact and website information for many of the resources, manufacturers, and related programs mentioned throughout this book.

Compass Manufacturers

The Brunton Co.
2255 Brunton Ct.
Riverton, Wyoming 82501
Phone: 307-857-4700
Website: www.brunton.com

Suunto Finland
Suunto Oy
Valimotie 7
FIN-01510 Vantaa
Finland
Phone: +358 9 875 870
Website: www.suunto.com

Geocaching.com Resources

Benchmark Hunting
www.geocaching.com/mark/

Cache In Trash Out
www.geocaching.com/CITO/

Geocaching in the News
www.geocaching.com/press/

Geocaching Software
www.geocaching.com/waypoints

GPS Adventures Maze
www.gpsmaze.com/

Groundspeak Forums
forums.groundspeak.com

Guide to Geocaching
www.geocaching.com/resources/guide_to_geocaching.pdf

GPS Manufacturers

The Brunton Co.
2255 Brunton Ct.
Riverton, Wyoming 82501
Phone: 307-857-4700
Website: www.brunton.com

Cobra Electronics
6500 West Cortland Street
Chicago, Illinois 60707
Phone: 773-889-3087
Website: www.cobra.com

DeLorme
Two DeLorme Drive
PO Box 298
Yarmouth, Maine 04096
Phone: 1-800-561-5105
Website: www.delorme.com

Garmin International
1200 E. 151st Street
Olathe, Kansas 66062
Phone: 1-800-800-1020
Website: www.garmin.com

Lowrance Electronics, Inc.
12000 E. Skelly Drive
Tulsa, Oklahoma 74128
Phone: 1-800-324-1354
Website: www.lowrance.com

Magellan Navigation Inc.
960 Overland Court
San Dimas, California 91773
Phone: 909-394-5000
Website: www.magellangps.com

Trimble Navigational Ltd.
935 Stewart Drive
Sunnyvale, California 94085
Phone: 1-800-874-6253
Website: www.trimble.com

Master list of GPS manufacturers
gauss.gge.unb.ca/manufact.htm

Geocaching Software

A list of software applications that support GPX and LOC file
formats.
www.geocaching.com/waypoints

ClayJar Watcher (GPX): Geocaching-specific freeware application
that helps you manage your Pocket Query GPX files.
www.clayjar.com/gc/watcher/

EasyGPS for Groundspeak (GPX/LOC): A great (free) application
for managing both LOC and GPX file types.
www.easygps.com/

Google Earth(GPX/KML): In addition to viewing caches via
Network KML, Google Earth can overlay the travels of trackable
items on geocaching.com. Google Earth also uses GPS Babel to
allow Premium Members the ability to drag a Pocket Query GPX
file on to the application to overlay geocaches.
www.googleearth.com

GPX Spinner (GPX): Geocaching-specific shareware application that can convert GPX files to iSolo and Plucker format.
www.gpxspinner.com/

GPSBabel (GPX/LOC/KML): A free console-based application for converting LOC and GPX to various other formats. Source code is available.
www.gpsbabel.org/

Geocaching Swiss Army Knife (GPX/LOC): A powerful and useful application that allows you to edit and combine GPX files and load them to your GPS and PDA.
www.gsak.net

GPS Connect for Mac OS X (GPX): Garmin-specific application that works with GPX.
www.chimoosoft.com/products/gpsconnect/

MacCaching Geocache Manager (GPX/LOC): A geocache manager for Mac OS X.
www.maccaching.com/

Trimble's Geocache Navigator: Fully featured geocaching application for mobile phones.
www.geocachenavigator.com

Groundspeak's Geocaching iPhone Application: Real-time access to Geocaching.com data with full geocaching capability.
www.geocaching.com/iphone/

GPS Software

DeLorme
PO Box 298
Yarmouth, Maine 04096
Phone: 1-800-452-5931
Website: www.delorme.com

Fugawi
95 St. Clair Avenue West, Suite 1406
Toronto, Ontario M4V 1N6 Canada
Website: www.fugawi.com

Maptech
10 Industrial Way
Amesbury, Maine 01913
Phone: 1-888-839-5551
Website: www.maptech.com

National Geographic Maps
375 Alabama Street, Suite 400
San Francisco, California 94110
Phone: 415-558-8700
Website: www.topo.com

OziExplorer
www.oziexplorer.com

TopoGrafix
PO Box 783
Medford, Maine 02155
Website: www.topografix.com

Map Resources

Google Maps
maps.google.com/

Microsoft Live Search
maps.live.com

TerraServer USA, Satellite photography
terraserver-usa.com

Trackmaker
www.gpstm.com

Yahoo Maps
maps.yahoo.com/

Newsgroups, Podcasts, and Zines

Cache-A-Maniacs—United States
www.cacheamaniacs.com/

Cache D' Island—Puerto Rico and the Caribbean
cdi.mypodcast.com/
(Spanish language)

Cachers of the Round Table—United States
www.cachersroundtable.com/

Centennial State Geocaching—Colorado, United States
centennialstategeocaching.com/

Dosen Fischer—Germany
www.dosenfischer.de/
(German language)

Geocaching Podcast—United States
www.geocachingpodcast.info/

Geocache Radio—Netherlands
www.geocacheradio.com/
(Dutch language)

Geocaching-Saglac.com—Canada
www.geocaching-saglac.com/
(French language)

Geotalk—Australia
geotalk.libsyn.com/

GPSInformation.net
gpsinformation.net/

GPS Magazine
www.gpsmagazine.com

Icenrye's Geocaching Videozine
www.icenrye.com/new/

Jersey Geocaching—New Jersey, United States
www.jerseygeocaching.com/

The Maine Podcache—Maine, United States
goddess.libsyn.com/

Ontario Geocaching Podcast—Canada
ontariogeocaching.podomatic.com/

PodCacher—United States
www.podcacher.com/

sci.geo.satellite-nav
www.gpsy.com/gpsinfo/gps-faq.html

Today's Cacher
www.todayscacher.com/

Twin Cities GeoCaching Podcast—Minnesota, United States
www.tcgcpc.com/

Paper Map Resources

Canada Map Office
Department of Energy, Mines, and Resources
615 Booth Street
Ottawa, Ontario K1A0E9 Canada
Phone: 1-800-465-6277

The Earth Science Information Center Headquarters
Phone: 1-800-USA-MAPS

Getty Thesaurus of Geographic Names
www.getty.edu/research/conducting_research/vocabularies/tgn

National Ocean Survey Map and Chart Information
Distribution Branch N/CG33
Riverdale, Maryland 20737
Phone: 303-436-6990

National Oceanic and Atmospheric Administration
1401 Constitution Avenue, NW
Room 5128
Washington, DC 20230
www.noaa.gov

U.S. Census Bureau
www.census.gov/cgi-bin/gazetteer

U.S. Geological Survey
507 National Center
Reston, Virgina 22092
Website: www.usgs.gov/

Related Activities

Armchair Treasure Hunt Club
www.treasureclub.net/

Bookcrossing.com
www.bookcrossing.com/

Canadian Money Tracker
www.cdn-money.ca/

The Degree Confluence Project
www.confluence.org/

EarthCaching
earthcache.org/

EuroBillTracker
en.eurobilltracker.com/

International Orienteering Organization
www.orienteering.org

Letterboxing North America
www.letterboxing.org/

Waymarking
www.waymarking.com/

Where's George?
www.wheresgeorge.com/

Where's Willy?
www.whereswilly.com/

Wherigo
www.wherigo.com

User-Generated Geocaching Tools

Geocacher University
www.geocacher-u.com/

Geochecker
www.geochecker.com/

It's Not About the Numbers
itsnotaboutthenumbers.com/

Team Markwell's GPS Adventures
www.markwell.us/geo.htm

Prime Suspect's Greasemonkey Scripts
gmscripts.locusprime.net/

Ranger Fox's Stat Bar Modifier
www.geocaching.com/profile/?u=ranger+fox

Weather

National Weather Service
www.nws.noaa.gov

The Weather Channel
www.weather.com

Almanac data   The information broadcast from GPS satellites used by the GPS receiver for computing its location.

ALR (Added Logging Requirement or **Additional Logging Requirement)**   Extra steps that the owner of a cache might ask of you in order to log his cache. They might include taking a picture or writing a poem. These are marked as mystery/puzzles even though they are usually at their posted coordinates. This is because they require the seeker to look at more than just the posted coordinates.

Altimeter   A gauge for measuring elevation.

Amateur radio   Also known as ham radio. Based on licensing privileges, various bands and frequencies are used for local, regional, or international communications. Handheld radios are 5 watts, but their range is substantial by transmitting through repeaters. Mobile radios are primarily 50 watts. (Compare that to CB radios, which are limited to only 4 watts.) A license is required through the FCC, but it is easy and inexpensive to obtain.

APRS (Automatic Position Reporting System)   GPS is combined with ham radios to provide mobile stations that are tracked by a computer using mapping software.

Archive   A cache that has been removed from the listings of Geocaching.com. The cache page is still available for review, but will not show up when searching for caches in an area. Geocaches are generally archived when they are missing, destroyed, or removed by the owner. Caches that simply need attention or repair are *"temporarily disabled"* rather than archived.

Attribute   One of a series of icons added to a geocache page that spells out any hazards, conditions, facilities, or other concerns about a cache.

Autorouting   GPS function that provides turn-by-turn directions to a waypoint. Directions may be in the form of arrows or automated voice commands.

Back bearing   Reversing a bearing for a return trip. It is 180 degrees in the opposite direction.

Baseline navigation   Baseline or handrail terrain features are linear reference points, such as roads, rivers, and power lines.

Bearing (BRG)   A direction measured by a compass degree needed to travel to stay on a course. Also known as an azimuth.

Benchmark hunting   The search for NGS (National Geodetic Survey) navigational survey markers. These markers document elevation or latitude/longitude points. Survey markers can be found with GPS or by following written instructions provided by the NGS.

Bison tube   A small, rust-proof cylindrical container with a watertight o-ring. These were designed to store pills but are often used for micro caches due to their size and durability.

Bookmark List   A feature for premium account members of Geocaching.com. Allows users to organize geocaches based on their own criteria.

Bureau of Land Management (BLM)   A U.S. government agency within the Department of the Interior. It manages 262 million acres of America's public lands, located primarily in 12 western states.

Cache   A shortened version of the word geocache. A container hidden that includes, at a minimum, a logbook for geocachers to sign.

Cardinal points   The primary compass points: N, E, S, and W. The intercardinal points are NE, SE, SW, and NW.

CITO (Cache In Trash Out)   An ongoing environmental initiative supported by the worldwide geocaching community. Geocachers bring trash bags with them and clean up the trails and parks by removing the trash that they find while geocaching.

Course   A direction traveled between two points, or to reach a destination.

Datum   A global survey system used to create maps. They are titled from the year they were created. Latitude and longitude are calculated differently for each datum. Geocaching uses the WGS 84 datum for all caches, although many maps still use NAD 27.

Decimal minutes   Geocaching uses this format of the latitude/longitude system, in which seconds are not shown. This is represented in the GPS receiver as HDDD° MM.MMM. HDDD stands for "hemisphere" and "degrees." MM.MMM stands for "minutes" in the decimal format.

Declination   The deference in degrees between magnetic north and true north.

DGPS (differential correction)   A system to improve GPS accuracy through ground-based radio transmitters to correct existing GPS signals for accuracy averaging 5 meters.

DNF (Did not find)   A term used by geocachers to state that they did not find a cache. This is also a type of online log on Geocaching. com and is useful for alerting cache owners of potential issues. A cache owner who repeatedly receives DNF logs should check to see that her cache has not been removed.

EPE number   The estimated position error number is based on satellite geometry with a reading that provides an estimate of accuracy in feet.

Estimated time en route (ETE)   The amount of time needed to reach the destination based on current speed and course.

Estimated time of arrival (ETA)   The time scheduled to arrive based on current speed and course.

Force (*The Force*)   The ability to instinctively know where a cache is hidden when you get within a certain proximity.

FTF (first to find) An acronym written by geocachers in physical cache logbooks or online when logging cache finds to denote being the first to find a new geocache.

Geocache A container hidden that includes, at a minimum, a logbook for geocachers to sign.

Geocaching A worldwide game of hiding and seeking treasure. A geocacher can place a geocache in the world, pinpoint its location using GPS technology, and then share the geocache's existence and location online.

Geocoin A small custom-minted coin that is used as a signature item for geocaching. Many geocoins are trackable at Geocaching. com, just like Travel Bug dog tags.

Global Positioning System (GPS) The global, satellite-based navigation system operated by the U.S. government. With the use of a GPS receiver, you can find your position anywhere in the world, and it is the basis for the game of geocaching.

GPSr A GPS receiver.

GPSr food A slang term for batteries.

Ground zero (GZ) The point when your GPS says you have arrived at the cache. Of course, that doesn't necessarily mean the cache hider's GPS agrees with yours.

Heading A marine term to describe a desired direction of travel.

Hitchhiker An item that is placed in a cache with instructions to relocate it to other caches. Sometimes they have logbooks attached so you can log their travels. Travel Bugs and geocoins are examples of hitchhikers.

Latitude/longitude system The world's primary navigational system, in which distances are measured in degrees, minutes, and seconds. Horizontal latitude lines measure north/south coordinates. Vertical longitude lines measure east/west coordinates.

Letterboxing A game similar to geocaching that started in the United Kingdom more than 100 years ago. The boxes are found by following clues and using a map and compass (www.letterboxing.org).

Magnetic   Direction of compass needle as it points to magnetic north.

Man overboard (MOB)   A GPS receiver function allowing a waypoint to be quickly saved in an emergency situation. This is typically done by holding down the GoTo button.

Markwelled   When a response to a new post in the online discussion forums points you to a similar topic discussed previously. Named after the resident archivist on the Geocaching.com discussion boards, Markwell.

Match safe   A small waterproof container designed to hold matches. They also make great micro cache containers.

Muggles   Also referred to as geo-muggles. A nongeocacher we meet in the field who wonders what we're doing, or someone who accidentally finds a cache. Based on the term "Muggle" (a nonmagical person) from the *Harry Potter* series. They are often puzzled looking, but are usually harmless.

National Marine Electronics Association (NMEA)   A universal electronic standard established to allow GPS, radios, and computers to exchange navigational data.

Nautical mile   6,080 feet, or 1.152 of a statute mile.

Navigation or "nav" target   The desired location or waypoint to be reached.

North grid   Vertical map grid lines that may deviate from true north.

Orienteering   A sport in which competitors race from point to point using a map and compass.

Pacing   A method of tracking distances by counting footsteps. A pace is one step. A stride is two steps, typically about 5 feet.

PDA   A personal digital assistant, such as a Palm Pilot.

Real-time tracking   A GPS receiver is connected to a computer loaded with mapping software. The user's current location is displayed on a computer screen as an icon centered on the digital-moving map.

ROT13   The encryption method utilized by the encrypted hints or logs on Geocaching.com.

Route   A series of waypoints listed in sequence from start to finish.

Selective availability (SA)   A degree of inaccuracy programmed by the U.S. government, causing civilian receivers to be off as much as 100 meters. SA was discontinued in May 2000.

Simulation mode   The format that allows the review and programming of information without the receiver attempting to search for satellites.

Spoiler   Text or photo that gives away too many details of a cache location, spoiling the experience for the next cachers who want to find it. Also used to describe a person who gives away details to other geocachers.

Statute mile   A standard ground mile with the distance of 5,280 feet. Established by the ancient Romans, its distance represented 5,000 Roman Legionnaire paces.

Terrain association   A way to orient a map to actual terrain by matching up prominent features and baseline features.

TFTC (Thanks for the cache)   An acronym written by geocachers in physical cache logbooks or online when logging cache finds.

The Degree Confluence Project   A GPS-based hobby involving visiting points where the latitude and longitude are integers (for example, N 42° 00.000 W 088° 00.000) and reporting your visit.

TNLN (Took nothing, left nothing)   Usually written in cache logbooks by geocachers who do not trade for material contents in a cache.

TNLNSL   Took nothing, left nothing, signed logbook.

TNSL   Took nothing, signed logbook.

Topographic or topo map   A detailed small-scale map showing elevation with contour lines.

Track (TRK)   The actual direction currently being traveled to reach a nav target.

Track log   An electronic breadcrumb trail that is stored and displayed by a GPS receiver, indicating a path traveled.

Trade items   The most commonly used term (after treasure) for items found in a cache.

Travel Bug   A special hitchhiker produced by Groundspeak, trackable on Geocaching.com.

Triangulation   Confirms a location by taking a bearing to more than one surrounding landmark. Effective in the field or on a map.

True   Direction to the actual North Pole.

UBBCode   UBBCode tags enable you to add formatting (bold, italics) and other information (e-mails, URLs) to your messages in the Geocaching.com online forums without learning HTML.

Universal time coordinated (UTC)   A universal time standard based on some point in the world. Many GPS receivers use the UTC at Greenwich, England.

Universal Transverse Mercator (UTM) system   The world's second primary navigation coordinate system. Often considered an easier system to use because it uses metric meters and kilometers instead of degrees, minutes, and seconds.

U.S. Forest Service (USFS)   A U.S. government agency of the Department of Agriculture. The USFS manages 191 million acres of national forests, grasslands, and prairies. These public lands are generally geocaching-friendly, except for designated wilderness areas, and other specially designated botanical, wildlife, and archaeological sites.

Variation   Another term for magnetic declination.

Watch list   A list of users on Geocaching.com who are watching a particular hitchhiker or cache. When a listing is logged, users on the watch list are notified by e-mail.

Waypoint   A selected point-of-interest location that can be saved, stored, and recalled from the GPS receiver's memory. Cache locations are saved as waypoints.

Wide-area augmentation system (WAAS)   Developed to improve GPS accuracy in the United States to within 3 meters 95 percent of the time through additional radio signals broadcast by 25 ground stations and two satellites.

Navigation and Map References

Distance

1 inch	25.4 millimeters	2.54 centimeters	
1 foot	12 inches	30.48 centimeters	
1 yard	3 feet	.914 meter	
1 mile (statute)	5,280 feet	1,760 yards	1.609 kilometers
1 nautical mile	6,080 feet	1,853 kilometers	1.15 of a mile
1 millimeter	.039 inch	.1 centimeter	
1 centimeter	.394 inch	10 millimeters	
1 meter	39.37 inches	3.28 feet	
1 kilometer	3,280.8 feet	.62 mile	1,000 meters
1 acre	43,560 sq. feet	approx. 208.7 feet	

Map Scales

1:500,000	1 inch = 8 miles
1:250,000	1 inch = 4 miles
1:150,000	1 inch = 2.4 miles
1:62,000 (15 minute)	1 inch = 1 mile
1:24,000 (7.5 minute)	1 inch = 2,000 feet (topo size)

UTM

Each grid is 1,000 meters (1 kilometer) square.

Latitude/Longitude

- Latitude lines run horizontally and measure north-south coordinates.

- Longitude lines run vertically, intersecting the poles to measure east-west coordinates.

- 1° (degree) = 60' (minutes), 1' (minute) = 60" (seconds).

- 1 degree = 69.05 statute miles = 111 kilometers.

- 1 minute = 1 nautical mile or 1.15 statute miles = 1.85 kilometers.

- 1 second = 100 feet = 30.83 meters.

Distances apply to latitude, but only to longitude at the equator.

Township, Range, Section

- A township equals 36 square miles.

- Each square mile is a section. Each section is numbered from 1 to 36. Section 1 begins in the northeast corner as the numbers proceed west, then east, alternately down each row, ending with 36 in the southeast corner.

- Each township has a township and range designation to define its 36-square-mile area.

- The horizontal rows are the township designation.

- The vertical rows are the range designation.

Sections are divided into quarters, which are further quartered to describe a property location: for example, SE 1/4, NW 1/4, Section 23, T.1 S., R.1 E., of the Salt Lake Base Line.

Geocaching Cache Log

GEOCACHING.COM

Geocache Name: _____

Placed by: _____

Contact Info: _____

Take something, leave something, sign the log.

Found by: _____ Date: _____
Notes:_____
_____
_____
_____

Found by: _____ Date: _____
Notes:_____
_____
_____
_____

Found by: _____ Date: _____
Notes:_____
_____
_____
_____

Found by: _____ Date: _____
Notes:_____
_____
_____
_____

Found by: _____ Date: _____
Notes:_____
_____
_____
_____

Found by: _____ Date: _____
Notes:_____
_____
_____
_____

GEOCACHE SITE—PLEASE READ

Congratulations, you've found it! Intentionally or not!

What is this hidden container sitting here for? What the heck is this thing doing here with all these things in it?

It is part of a worldwide game dedicated to GPS (Global Positioning System) users, called Geocaching. The game basically involves a GPS user hiding "treasure" (this container and its contents), and publishing the exact coordinates so other GPS users can come on a "treasure hunt" to find it. The only rules are: if you take something from the cache, you must leave something for the cache, and you must write about your visit in the logbook. Hopefully, the person that hid this container found a good spot that is not easily found by uninterested parties. Sometimes, a good spot turns out to be a bad spot, though.

IF YOU FOUND THIS CONTAINER BY ACCIDENT:

Great! You are welcome to join us! We ask only that you:

- Please do not move or vandalize the container. The real treasure is just finding the container and sharing your thoughts with everyone else who finds it.

- If you wish, go ahead and take something. But please also leave something of your own for others to find, and write it in the logbook.

- If possible, let us know that you found it, by visiting the website listed below.

Geocaching is open to everyone with a GPS and a sense of adventure. There are similar sites all over the world. The organization has its home on the Internet. Visit our website if you want to learn more, or have any comments:

www.geocaching.com

If this container needs to be removed for any reason, please let us know. We apologize, and will be happy to move it.

Travel Itinerary

Critical Information to Leave Behind

❑ Ranger Station   ❑ Family/Friends   ❑ At Trailhead

Trip Date & Time: _____ Return Date & Time: _____

Destination: _____

Geocache(s): _____

Location Description: _____

Route Taken:_____

_____

Coordinates: _____

Motels/Campgrounds: _____

Comm. Ham: Frequencies _____ Cell (   ) _____

Sat. Ph. (   ) _____ CB: Ch. 1 _____ Ch. 2 _____ FM: _____

Person(s):

Name _____ Contact Phone _____

_____

_____

Vehicle(s):

Make _____ Model _____

Color _____ License Plate _____

Photocopy this page courtesy of Alpha Books

Gear Checklist

For Geocaching, Camping, and Outdoor Adventure

- ❏ Ax
- ❏ Batteries
- ❏ Binoculars
- ❏ Camera and film or digital storage media
- ❏ Clothing, two sets minimum
- ❏ Cooking kit and utensils
- ❏ Dog stuff, including food
- ❏ Energy bars
- ❏ Firewood
- ❏ Flashlights and batteries
- ❏ Glasses, contacts
- ❏ GPS and accessories
- ❏ Insect repellent
- ❏ Licenses (game)

- ❏ Bar-B-Q or grill
- ❏ Beverages
- ❏ Boots and socks
- ❏ Cell, 2-way, CB
- ❏ Compass
- ❏ Cooler and ice
- ❏ Emergency blanket
- ❏ Fire extinguisher
- ❏ First-aid/snakebite ki
- ❏ Gas and oil
- ❏ Gloves
- ❏ Hat
- ❏ Jackets (light/heavy)
- ❏ Kid stuff

❏ Knife, large and small

❏ Maps, general and top

❏ Money: cash/credit cards/ traveler checks

❏ Passport

❏ Rope

❏ Signal mirror and whistle pillows

❏ Snow chains

❏ Sun block, lip balm

❏ Swimwear

❏ Tent

❏ Toolbox

❏ Water

❏ _____

❏ _____

❏ _____

❏ _____

❏ _____

❏ _____

❏ Lantern and fuel

❏ Medication

❏ Notepad and pencil

❏ Propane gas

❏ Shovel

❏ Sleeping bags and

❏ Stove and fuel

❏ Sunglasses

❏ Tarp

❏ Toiletries

❏ Toothbrush and paste

❏ Waterproof matches

❏ _____

❏ _____

❏ _____

❏ _____

❏ _____

❏ _____

❑ Meals:

Breakfast: _____

_____

_____

Lunch: _____

_____

_____

Dinner: _____

_____

_____

Snacks: _____

_____

_____

Photocopy these pages courtesy of Alpha Books

Index

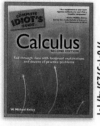